The Achiever's Journey

by

Genevieve Dawid

*Dyslexia is a gift and not a stigma!
Sent with love
from
Genevieve Dawid.*

Acknowledgements

To push open my door of opportunity for this special book, I enlisted the support of some special people.

My heartfelt thanks go to my great 'team' who travelled with me on this fascinating journey as I wrote 'The Achiever's Journey'. It truly has been a global affair.

Cover design – *Ricardo Insua-Cao - Vietnam/UK*
PDF layout - *Dave Lovitt - Graphit England*
Web site design - *David Lakins, Key multimedia - England*
Editing - *Joti Bryant - Canada*

Last but not least, my wonderful husband, Richard, who supported and assisted me through the thousands of hours spent on the book. My writing took place in many different locations, including: the Azores, the West Indies, Europe and whilst crossing the Atlantic.

I couldn't have achieved it without you all.

In memory of my Mum and Dad

Who encouraged me to
"Push open the door
of opportunity"!

Your ever loving daughter

Genevieve

Mentoring Courses

For more information on Mentoring courses

By Genevieve Dawid

Either One to One mentoring,

Interactive Workshops, Seminars

or courses held in wonderful locations worldwide

View our website at

www.theachieversjourney.com

Keynote speeches

For more information on keynote speeches

by Genevieve Dawid

View our website at

www.genevievedawid.com

Contents

Introduction		7
Chapter one	The Beginning	9
Chapter two	Explaining the Journey	13
Chapter three	Using your own map	23
Chapter four	Charting your course	43
Chapter five	Changing position	65
Chapter six	Making good progress	87
Chapter seven	Being organised	107
Chapter eight	Keep up the performance	131

© Copyright 2007 Genevieve Dawid
All rights reserved. No part of this publication may be reproduced, stored in a retrieval system, or transmitted, in any form or by means, electronic, mechanical, photocopying, recording, or otherwise, without the written permission of the author.

A catalogue record for this title is available from the British Library. www.bl.uk

ISBN 978-0-9556529-0-5

This edition published 2007 by LGD Management – Publishing Division,
London, United Kingdom

Printed and bound by Hobbs the Printers Ltd, Totton, Hampshire, United Kingdom
Printed on 50% recycled paper

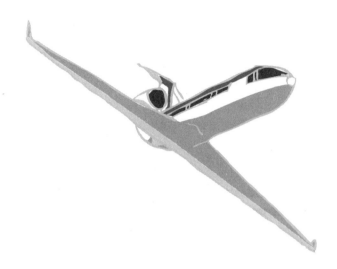

Introduction

The fact that you picked up this book and are open to investigating new ways to move positively forward in your life, says something about you as a person...

You're a winner because you took the initiative to achieve something new!

You were intuitive enough to explore what lies before you: a book that can assist you to develop powerful new skill sets – which will enable you to materialise your dreams, realise your full potential and improve your lifestyle.

Within these pages you will travel on an exciting journey of self-discovery and expansion; discover your unique strengths and abilities, and acquire valuable tools and resources to overcome any obstacles along the way.

The methods and guidance that follow result from my own personal life challenges from early childhood, and a need

Introduction

to find new ways of functioning, in order to cope with daily life.

I will share with you the learning gifts I inherited from my parents, (which I subsequently went on to develop), which helped me in so many ways, and later, other people. With these tools, I re-educated my peers at school, students at world-famous universities, colleagues at work, and over the past few years, those at the top of the corporate ladder.

After overcoming certain difficulties which I came into this life with, I am now a professional business and personal mentor (or guide). My role is to take you safely from where you are now, to where you want to be.

Thousands of people have benefited from this unique blend of mentoring - based on what takes place during actual mentoring sessions.

You will progress with your own virtual map - a blueprint for your life. This will help give you the route to a future, you might only have imagined.

This is one journey where you, the Driver, always remain in complete control…

If you are ready to go forward and achieve, The Achiever's Journey will allow you to push open your own doors of opportunity.

Let the journey begin!

Genevieve Dawid

Templates of The Achiever's Journey exercises are available through the website

www.theachieversjouney.com

Chapter One

The Beginning

The door of opportunity has got 'Push!' written all over it!
-My Father

Success is whatever you deem it to be!

Thankfully we are all unique! We come from different backgrounds, with different aspirations and goals.

This book has been designed to take you on a very special journey, one that will enable you to create a brighter and more fulfilling future.

If you didn't have the perfect start in life (not many people do!) or feel that your past hasn't led you where you wanted to be today, don't worry, you can still progress and realise your full potential.

Chapter One - The Beginning

Maybe you just want to acquire better habits or organisational skills, these too can be achieved through The Achiever's Journey.

It is my privilege to be your guide, and accompany you throughout this wonderful voyage. As we will be travelling companions, I will explain a bit about the philosophy behind my work as a mentor, which comes from my own early life.

I was born dyslexic, dyspraxic, had my feet the wrong way round, and put up for adoption at one month old. Luckily, I gained wonderful new parents when I was just six weeks old.

As a child, putting my feet in the right direction was relatively easy, compared to trying to understand the way my brain worked! But with love and support I have achieved many things in my life.

My parents were instrumental in my success. They accepted me exactly as I was, and always believed in me. They loved and cared for me, and always had my best interests at heart; I could not have wished for a better start. And with great patience, they worked hard to understand, and help me through my early learning difficulties.

As I grew older, I developed some of my parents' teachings to invent my own ways of coping, to get to know myself better, discover where I was, and where I wanted to go in life. I was fortunate that my parents also taught me to be positive and to always look forward, never sideways or down. They taught me to love and accept myself, encouraging me never to feel inferior, and to develop my own special gifts.

We are all blessed with different gifts and possess different skill sets, and we must learn how to embrace them for our own good, and not regret the ones we may be missing.

Chapter One - The Beginning

Although I am dyslexic, I communicate well and am highly perceptive. It took time but eventually I learned to read and write very well, to the point where I began writing books. It is widely known that dyslexics have highly developed skills in other areas, to compensate, and many are highly successful entrepreneurs.

Throughout my childhood, my parents had to keep reassessing my development and invent new ways of learning for me. As each learning difficulty presented itself, my parents didn't give up, instead they devised new strategies to enable me to progress.

However, once I learned something, it was mine forever. Eventually, with perseverance, I caught up with my peer group, in most areas of my education.

With the benefit of my parents' learning strategy, by the time I was eighteen I had made great strides forward, achieved my qualifications and I was ready, excited and equipped, to go out into the big wide world and achieve my dreams.

But there was to be a bizarre twist. A week after my eighteenth birthday, my wonderful and intelligent Mum, who had always found learning so easy and had devoted so much energy to helping me to learn, suddenly collapsed and went into a coma. She was hospitalised and diagnosed with a large brain tumour. After life-saving surgery, she was a shadow of her former self. We were all totally devastated.

Now the tables had turned and I was using Mum's strategies to overcome her own never-ending stream of daily challenges. I can't tell you how hard those days were; as an eighteen-year-old girl I had to grow up fast, to cope with caring medically, physically and mentally for her. Every day I identified and solved problems related to her condition; believe me, there are endless difficulties in

Chapter One - The Beginning

looking after someone so ill.

Over the years Mum developed two further brain tumours but amazingly, with her ever-positive attitude, had another eleven years of life. She travelled extensively, lived life to the full, and achieved her dream to see her first grandchild born, my daughter, whom she adored. Throughout her later years my father took on the caring role, and we continued our family philosophy of loving, caring for, and supporting each other, in whatever ways we could. I am told, had Mum developed her brain tumours now, that with the great medical advances that have taken place, she would have survived. Such is life!

The philosophy I gained from my parents has benefited not only my family, but thousands of others; just like a seed it has grown and developed. And it will spread even further now, as I have the pleasure of sharing it with you, for your own benefit.

In my work as a consultant and mentor, my parents' attitude has helped me to always have my clients' best interests at heart, and to support them through obstacles, both in their careers and personal lives. Because I genuinely care about the people I work with, wanting to understand them and always accepting who they are, many people have come to me for help.

Now it is time to move on, next I will explain the journey to you.

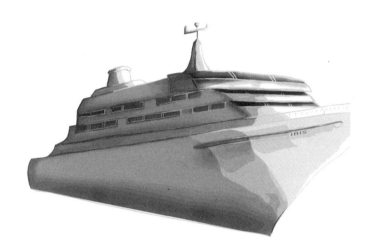

Chapter Two

Explaining the Journey

If I had my life to live over, I would have had more actual trouble but fewer imaginary ones, eat more ice cream and less beans.
— Nadine Stair, aged 85

Our lives are one long journey, from beginning to end, and during them we have many other journeys. Looking back, we can view these as the different chapters of our lives. Inevitably, life presents problems for us to deal with, many unforeseen, and we have to deal with these the best way we can.

The Achiever's Journey is not just mentoring for short-term individual goals. My intention, or wish, is for you to learn ways of creating long-term disciplines and habits, to enable you to not only continually achieve what you desire in all areas of your life, but to also more effectively handle any problems, as they arise.

This journey is open to everyone...

For those of you who want to improve your career or current position, also included in the book are mentoring tips based on my professional experience in assessing personnel, and search/selection procedures. These are ideas that you can use to create ways to move your career forward, or improve your present circumstances or future working conditions.

When you experience any sudden or unexpected life change, such as redundancy or illness, or find that your life or career isn't going in the right direction, that's the time to find some help to get re-motivated and discover new ways forward.

The Achiever's Journey involves taking steps forward to implement your goals, creating your own new chapters - so you can live your life to the full - in your own special way.

Now you can start to really know and understand yourself, learn what you truly want for your future, prepare and implement important changes in your life, create new habits, allow yourself to evolve, track your successes and develop/nurture the future that you have chosen.

This is **your** personal Achiever's Journey. You will receive virtual personal mentoring. I will guide you through exactly the same process and stages of progression that you would experience if we were to work together in person.

Life is full of choices, and you can choose them, consciously.

The progression of input and motivation that we received throughout our childhood and early adulthood tends to

Chapter Two - Explaining the Journey

slow down after finishing our education, thus as we get older, we can so easily get stuck in a rut, or lose our way.

Unless we continue to stretch and nurture ourselves, by seeking advice from trusted sources, continue our education, and consistently find ways to stimulate our minds and creativity, we stop developing. I believe that good mentoring also provides continual personal growth, helping us as we encounter new areas in our lives.

Over the years, many people have come to me for help, to redirect their career paths, improve their working relationships, or when they were stuck in a rut. I have worked with a wide range of clients: from people who are highly successful to those who feel broken and have lost their way.

What I can tell you — based on my experience – is that you too can achieve. You just need to have the will, the inclination, and be prepared to allocate the time. Though I should warn you, at times during The Achiever's Journey process clients say they have 'brain ache' as they work through the exercises! Don't worry, that's fine, just what we want. I need to make you think, and be able to understand yourself, using these new pathways.

Another key point I would like you to be aware of is that a lot of clients who go through my course often end up, (through their own choice), in a very different place to where they initially thought they were going. This is quite normal, during the journey you will naturally change and evolve, and what you desire may change too.

This book will act as a catalyst for your ongoing personal development. You might also want to review your current job situation, explore future developments in your career, or assess other areas in your life.

Unfortunately, sometimes in life there can seem to be a void, or you reach a plateau. During these periods it may be difficult to identify what it is that you want, or perceive what stage you are currently at in your life.

With the help of a mentor, acting as a professional advisor or third party, you can assess your current situation and clarify what you need to focus on, then decide upon the actions you need to take next to move forward.

The Achiever's Journey is a way for you to realistically accomplish your goals. After learning my philosophy and structure, you will be able to retain what you learn, including new disciplines or habits, for life.

What I am offering is a blueprint for achieving what you want, one that can be used right now, and for all the changes you may wish to make in your future. You can repeat this journey for each new event in your life, or simply as a 'refresher'.

I have a wonderful career, one that I thoroughly enjoy, and it still has a long way to go. What I enjoy most is helping the fascinating people I work with to achieve their dreams.

For a long time I wanted to extend my work to help a larger audience, and I can now share all that I have learnt with you. This book was written to provide genuine help and guidance. Within it I share some of my own life experiences, my philosophy, and a time-proven structure, to mentor and benefit you.

Along the way, I will share the knowledge I have gained through helping hundreds of people in my mentoring role. Where it may help, I will also share with you some of my own personal life experiences.

People ask me what it is that makes my mentoring so successful. I tell them that there are three main things:

1. ***I help you think more clearly, and understand yourself better.***

Chapter Two - Explaining the Journey

    2. I talk and mentor from my experience, not from a text book or preconceived ideas.

    3. I don't mentor for a 'quick fix' but educate you for a life-time of achieving.

Professionally, I have a decade of first hand experience and knowledge in this field, through working both on a one-to-one basis and in groups, for corporations and professional institutions.

Although primarily my experience is from working with senior management and professionals, the same philosophy and mentoring works equally well with all types of people, including youngsters, undergraduates, those who have temporally lost their way in life and basically anyone who has the desire to achieve more.

As your mentor I am not here to tell you what to do.

My aim is to help you to help yourself, so that you have more control in your life.

Mentoring

A personal mentor is someone who cares about you, someone you can trust, and someone who can help you develop your potential.

Each mentor has their own unique way of working; mine is based on both my own personal background and my professional experience with all types of people.

Even if the idea of a mentor is new to you, you have already experienced mentoring in your life, though you may not have been aware of it. For example, when you were a child mentoring through guidance was provided by those who cared for you; from your parents, siblings, teachers, or other adults who helped you develop. As you got older it probably continued with further education, from elders, friends or managers in your job.

Chapter Two - Explaining the Journey

Individuals within national and local government, international organisations such as the United Nations, senior managers of companies or corporations - in fact key people in any large organisations - all have advisors/ mentors for policy changes.

My first mentors were my new parents, who adopted me as a baby.

In the greater scheme of things my problems weren't serious, but created daily challenges for me.

My mental development was quite slow and I didn't utter a word until after the age of two. I couldn't read or understand words or numbers in any definite order - something I didn't master until I was about eight. I wasn't able to put my shoes on the correct feet till I was nearly nine, tie my shoe laces until I was eleven, and was thirteen before I could properly tell the time. I just found learning difficult.

Like most good things this philosophy is simple, yet very effective. And if you have the will, then I have the way to help you.

Your own journey is a very personal one. Together we will, on your time clock and at your pace, carefully prepare, start the journey, travel together, deal with any obstacles or diversions along the way, stop for mechanical services, and re-fuel when necessary. I'll also give you information on how to stay on course, and also, celebrate your successes!

When we look to achieve something new, we are usually looking to build on past success, change direction, or get out of a situation we feel stuck in. When I mentor you, I will make you stop and think, and encourage you to allow your thoughts to flow.

It's a good idea to give some thought before you start and to be clear about what you want from each particular journey.

Chapter Two - Explaining the Journey

Any journey needs forethought, planning, preparation, a map, and someone in the driver's seat, YOU.

As your mentor I will be your constant companion, helping to keep you on track, and acting as navigator where needed. I will accompany you to help you reach your chosen destination. Should you require them, we will pick up other supporting passengers as we travel: voice coach, health practitioner, fitness instructor - whatever fits your needs.

Professional mentoring is about helping you to understand, plan and implement whatever it is that you want to achieve. My philosophy is successful because it is based on tried-and-tested methods. It's not hype, but a no-nonsense approach to achievement. It doesn't need to be made complicated.

I offer a realistic, positive, safe environment, to enable you to grow and develop at your own pace, and at the time that is right for you.

Mentoring becomes far easier when structured, so I have developed a map for The Achiever's Journey, which has worked very well for my clients, and will work for you. It doesn't matter whether you are at the very top of your career or just starting out, trying to improve yourself or considering a lifestyle change, the map works for anyone with a sincere desire to achieve more.

I want to assure you that my formula will allow you to get what you want out of mentoring. As you go through the process, some aspects, chapters or exercises will be more relevant and important for you than others and you can adjust the level of commitment you give to each section.

In this book I have provided tried-and-tested exercises for you to identify your own challenges, and get to know yourself - which is the key to making informed judgements about your future.

Timing – Using this journey effectively

To get the most out of your journey, you will need time, motivation and commitment. If you are looking for inspiration, new disciplines and habits, and have time and the desire, this is your vehicle to achieve these things.

The great benefit of my system is that you can do as little, or as much, as you want, and at your own pace. Remember, the smallest of achievements can start the ball rolling.

Just reading this book, or doing one of the exercises is an achievement!

Timing is very important to your success. If you are ready to make serious changes and progress in the near future, you need to choose a time when you are going to be able to put things in place. It could be after a holiday, Christmas, your birthday, the first of the month - or maybe even today. Just decide upon the right starting date for you, and then you can begin.

Please read the book whenever you feel drawn to it, and use whatever parts or tools within it that feel right for you at the time.

Chapter Two - Explaining the Journey

Progress Report:

You have now progressed by:

- ❏ *knowing more about the journey you want to take*
- ❏ *discovering how a personal mentor can help you develop your potential*
- ❏ *understanding that to get the most out of your journey you will need to devote time, be motivated and committed*
- ❏ *learning the benefits of mentoring: to think in new ways, and get to know yourself better*
- ❏ *knowing that you remain in the driving seat, retain full control at all times and travel at your own pace*
- ❏ *comprehending the philosophy behind my successful mentoring, which may include enlisting other people to provide support*

Chapter Two - Explaining the Journey

Chapter Three - Using your own map

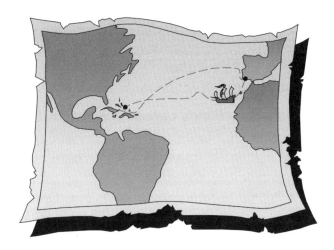

Chapter Three

Using your own map

If you travel a path without obstacles it probably doesn't lead anywhere

– Frank A Clark

Your Journey

I use the structure of a map for my mentoring, which you will personally create for each journey, using the tools in this book.

Before starting, you choose the vehicle you wish to travel in, or you may prefer to walk with me, side-by-side, as I navigate, guide and support you throughout the trip.

Chapter Three - Using your own map

You can choose the intensity of your unique journey and make it simple or challenging as you like, especially if you are looking to develop a complete new lifestyle. It has been my experience that those who come to me saying that they are going to change or improve their lifestyle or careers do so, and those who say "well", "maybe" or "perhaps", find it an awful lot harder.

I'm not saying that change happens overnight, but it **really** helps if you have a positive attitude - based on reality.

Be realistic

It is best to be realistic during your Achiever's Journey.

Any journey of discovery is exciting. Just imagine what interesting things and people you might come across... But be honest, when you start off on a journey in real life, do you always have a straightforward journey with absolutely no hitches or obstacles?

Have you ever set off on a trip and not had to stop for red stop lights? Never been diverted by road-works, or affected by bad weather? Probably not.

When you take a journey and the traffic lights change to red, or your flight is delayed, you don't say, "Right that's it, I've had enough. All those people in front of me got though on the green light (my plane is delayed), and now I'm feeling so depressed I'm going home and giving up on the whole journey!"

The truth is that when you take a journey of any kind you have to be realistic. To reach your destination you will not find the journey without some hitches, so why should this journey to achieve be any different?

Like other journeys though, it's always a great feeling and worthwhile when you arrive at your destination.

Chapter Three - Using your own map

This is a wonderful opportunity; a wonderful path lies before you. Embrace, enjoy, and learn from it - to create a brighter future.

My Five-Point Philosophy

My mentoring philosophy is based on my parents' original ways of helping me, which were very simple but highly effective. Over the years I have developed and expanded upon these five principles.

One

Identify Problems and Areas Needing Improvement

The first step is finding and identifying the problem(s) you need to deal with. This is something most individuals can't see for themselves, and in corporate life especially, with so many people and personalities to deal with, it is sometimes difficult to perceive what's going on in every area.

Two

Plan Your Goals

Once the problems and areas for improvements are uncovered or recognised then you can set your goals in order of importance: short, medium, and long-term. This list of goals can be amended as and when you like, because you are in total control.

Three

Create and Implement a Strategy

Once the goals are listed and prioritised you need to have a strategy to implement them.

Realistically, not every strategy works first time. To improve yourself, or your life, you simply need to devise new strategies, as and when required.

When you see these strategies start to work and change your life, it's a wonderful experience!

Four

Track and Record Results

It is vital to record and monitor your changes. One of the greatest motivators is tracking your results, which allows you to observe your progress, and see how you are constantly building upon your successes.

I use a Record of Achievements regularly; it constantly reminds me of what I have achieved thus far. Memories are relived and the inspiration becomes a catalyst for the next task.

Five

Keep Going

The key is not to let obstacles get in your way and to keep pressing ahead. Pay little attention to any negative thoughts or setbacks you may encounter, just stay focused on your progress and remind yourself of past successes.

I discovered, (and more importantly, **decided**), early on, when faced with so many challenges, that nothing would remain a permanent obstacle in my life. I knew I could deal with any future problems, as they came along.

It isn't that I no longer struggle or face daily challenges now, but I do try to keep moving forward.

My Aunt Janet, had Downs Syndrome. I think some of Mum's creative ways of getting me to learn might have been based on her experience of her sister's learning difficulties.

Janet was a great inspiration to me, demonstrating that we all have potential, we just need to be in the right environment and frame of mind to achieve and keep going forward.

Chapter Three - Using your own map

Just look around you to discover and then appreciate those you can learn from, or be inspired by. We can gain inspiration from everyone around us, if we will only look for the positive qualities within them.

Experience has also shown me that those who weren't fortunate enough to have good nurturing in their formative years can still achieve. Good adult nurturing can also be very effective and can help to replace or eliminate early negative input.

It is never too late, we are always evolving and changing, the key is to always keep an open mind.

Chapter Three - Using your own map

The Exercises

I have re-created some of the exercise templates on The Achiever's Journey website:

> www.theachieversjourney.com

In this book I have re-created the most frequently used and most successful exercises I use with my clients.

The exercises will help you focus on your own achievements, true feelings and emotions, and discover where you are in your life. They will work perfectly, but only if you have an open mind and you are honest with yourself.

Clients often say they are taken aback at times by the revelations and insights gained through the exercises.

Some of you will read the book and then do the exercises, others will do them as you go along. It doesn't matter either way. This is your journey and you travel as you see fit.

Sometimes during these exercises you might find yourself feeling stuck, or blocked, and that is quite common. Just give yourself some time or even go away and come back to it. Often your brain already knows the answers but your conscious mind just hasn't caught up. If you let your mind be free-flowing and don't strain to find the answers, then they will come automatically. Once I have asked you a question, the seed is planted and your unconscious mind is working for you.

If at any time your answers to the exercises surprise or confuse you, don't worry, allow your mind to be free and re-adjust. The exercises are there to make you think and review your opinions. Give yourself time. Travel through the exercises in this book at your own pace. You are in complete control.

You will start to discover that what you draw or write down is a good indicator or representation of what you really feel, but may be quite different to what you tell yourself, or expect. Please don't worry about how you feel about your drawings or writing, you will soon feel at ease with them and welcome this new tool in your life.

These exercises are aimed at starting to make you think in a new way and will help you reflect your thoughts on paper. The results will be personal to you

I suggest you do the drawing and writing exercises in pencil to allow you to amend and add to them as more ideas come to you.

1. *Take time to relax and think. Set aside time for yourself.*
2. *Let your thoughts flow freely and put them straight down onto paper.*
3. *Either draw straight onto the allocated page in this book, or use your notebook or A4 folder.*
4. *Don't be concerned if you can't interpret your writing and drawings straight away, eventually you will discover what they mean.*
5. *Continue doing the exercises you want to do - when you are in the right frame of mind to do them.*

Your private notebook

You may choose to use this book to do your exercises. Personally I have found notebooks (or A4 ring binders) very useful. When mentoring in person, some clients share the contents of their exercises with me, some never reveal any of it or just a part, which is fine. There are not many places in the world where you can have total privacy these days, but your notebook can be one of them.

Chapter Three - Using your own map

A notebook can have many uses. You can use it as a place where you can be free and totally honest about your thoughts, feelings, goals and actions. The notebook can also be a way to write about and to release feelings of anger, sadness, happiness, or any emotion you are experiencing at any particular time. You will also find that the discipline of writing down or using drawings to record and track your thoughts is useful for all areas of your life.

To protect your privacy I suggest that you don't write your name on your notebook. Choose a distinctive, special notebook that you will enjoy using.

At any time, you can re-read this permanent record of your inner thoughts and the exercises of this journey.

It is helpful periodically to go back and review previous notes and exercises, to see the progress and achievements you have recorded – your own personal diary. I recently reviewed notes and exercises from ten years ago and I can't believe what I thought then, and also the extent to which I have changed, evolved and progressed…

Based on my clients' comments, I also recommend that you use the back of your notebook for jotting down useful details: networking names, addresses, and contact information, that you can refer back to. You can then input the material later into a computer or as a hard copy if you wish.

Tracking

Tracking is a way of following the progress of your goals and achievements after implementing them. Basically it allows you to record your results, but tracking is also vital to your success on this journey.

My example is a simple one, something that could be used for work, although you can use tracking for any area of your life.

Let's say your goal is to achieve 8 sales a week in your job. First write down your goal, then record what you actually achieve. The table below gives one example of how it can be set up.

Example -

Corporate Sales Tracking List

	Target	Achieved
Wk 1	3 Sales	3 Sales
Wk 2	4 Sales	5 Sales
Wk 3	5 Sales	4 Sales
Wk 4	6 Sales	7 Sales
Wk 5	8 Sales	8 Sales

Tracking is a wonderful tool for keeping you motivated. It gives you an incentive, as you can physically see where you are being successful, and that's something we all love to do. You can apply the principle of tracking your progress to any aspect of your life.

Some of the exercises in this book require tracking results, where applicable I have added tables for you to record these tracking results.

I strongly suggest that you use your notebook or A4 ring binder for tracking, alternatively put the information in your diary or note pad, or even make a chart and put it up on the wall. It's not how you track it, but the fact that you are tracking achievements that's important. Just thinking you are doing well does not have the same impact as keeping a record, as your mind responds better to a written (visual) statement.

How the structure works -Your own map

This is your personal imaginary map, as you see it in your own mind, and entirely your own creation. Your map might have paths, cycle lanes, single-track lanes, lakes and streams, motorways, hills and valleys, train tracks, or shipping lanes. It can be below sea level, or have endless corridors. Whatever you like can be added, it's entirely your choice. Soon we will draw the starting point of your map. First we need to discuss what method of transport you would like to use or of course you may prefer to be on foot.

Choice of transport

To start your journey, choose just one method of transport. This can be any kind of transport you like, from a tank to your dream sports car, from a train to a plane. Or you may even want to walk beside me. Whatever you choose you will remain safe at all times and we shall share this journey together.

Here are some suggestions to get you started:

* *Car / 4 x 4 / sports car / SUV*

* *Tank / armoured vehicle*

* *Jet ski / hang glider*

* *Bicycle / motorbike*

* *Train*

* *Plane / glider / rocket*

* *Ship / yacht / canoe*

* *Walking - travelling on foot on a coastal path or through the countryside*

Whatever method of transportation you choose will be right for you at the start of your journey. If you are feeling

Chapter Three - Using your own map

fragile then you may well choose a tank because you may think that they are very safe and my tanks will provide you with 100% protection. If you don't want an ordinary tank you could have one with leather interior and power-assisted steering. If you can imagine it, then it exists for this journey.

The nice thing is that at any time you can choose something different. If you start off in a tank and then feel more confident, you could change to a plane or a train. If you start off with a Porsche Cabriolet then hit bad weather, you could change to a four-by-four, and later switch to a Rolls Royce.

You can also have a pit-stop at any point to alter your type of vehicle, or just take a break.

Fuel

I will provide any materials: water, oil, windscreen cleaner, spare tyres, whatever your particular needs. What you provide is the fuel to progress forward. It can only come from you; it is your energy and your effort that makes that fuel priceless.

When I want to achieve something, I take a journey, just like the one I have described, and the one that you are about to set off on. I usually start off in a tank, then fly, and end up in a great car for my onward journey.

Chapter Three - Using your own map

Example - Draw your starting point

It's now time for you to draw a picture of your starting point on your imaginary map, using whatever mode of transport and environment that reflects your starting position. To make it clearer, here are some examples:

Example 1

Example 2

Draw your starting position

Now draw a picture of the method of transport that suits your starting position/current mood.

Chapter Three - Using your own map

The Journey – Work in Action (Case study)

On this journey you must also be prepared to adapt to changing conditions.

For example, I had a client who wanted to become Managing Director/ Chief Executive Officer (MD/CEO) for the company he was currently working for. To do that he needed to improve his personal life, update his Curriculum Vitae (CV) and work on his presentation skills. His preparation was good. The choice of vehicle to start with was a fast sports car. Within a couple of days disaster struck in the form of a 'business tornado'. The MD/CEO position that he had applied for was now to be split into two, and the salary would be drastically reduced.

The client contacted me and I helped him find a strategy. This was the time to evolve and adapt. This client decided to quickly change his transport to a plane as he decided to move from his existing company to seek MD/CEO positions elsewhere. Luckily, he had updated his CV and references and improved his skill sets and better organised himself. This meant he could now fly off somewhere new as quickly as he desired. Soon he was going for first interviews for MD/CEO positions in other companies.

Eventually he achieved the perfect job position and so for his onward journey he went back to the fancy sports car. The imaginary virtual map gave this client energy, and when he needed to up his game he could imagine seeing himself going from the fancy sports car on the open road, to flying at great speed, to wherever he needed to go.

Identifying problems, difficulties and bad habits

When I am mentoring, either on a one-to-one basis, or in my workshops, seminars or lectures - I usually start by helping identify problems or difficulties, and/or bad habits to be changed. Then we look at what short, medium and long-term goals the client wants to achieve, or areas they want to improve.

So start by listing any problems, difficulties, bad habits, or anything that you want to change or improve. Give yourself enough time to create this list.

List any problems, difficulties, bad habits you wish to change and improvements you would like to make

Chapter Three - Using your own map

Your initial starting goals

I will provide you with a lot to think about as we progress.

Looking at your list of problems, difficulties, bad habits, and changes or improvements that you want to make, we will start by turning this list into your initial goals. These goals may well change and evolve as we proceed through the journey, you will keep referring back to them.

This list of goals can be changed any time, but for now, list below your goals for the short, medium and long-term. Be realistic with the number of goals you wish to implement in the short-term. Remember it is better to achieve one goal than struggle with five.

As the journey moves along, you can move goals around. For example you might find a long-term goal ends up in the short-term list. For that reason you may prefer to do this exercise in pencil in the table overleaf.

Chapter Three - Using your own map

My Initial Goals

Short-term goals

Medium-term goals

Long-term goals

Progress Report:

You are doing really well, so far you have:

- ***understood that life is a journey and The Achiever's Journey is the way to create positive chapters within it.***
- ***understood that the structure for your journey is a map.***
- ***created your starting point for a new journey by visualising and drawing your own map, and selecting the type of transport you wish to use.***
- ***put in place your essential tool kit, pen/pencil notebook and/or A4 ring-binder***
- ***spent time identifying your difficulties, bad habits, and anything you want to improve and change.***
- ***compiled from this list the initial short, medium and long-term goals that you want to achieve, and know that you can alter these at any point in the journey.***

Chapter Three - Using your own map

Chapter Four - Charting your course

Chapter Four

Charting your course

The most difficult matter isn't to change the world, but yourself.
— Nelson Mandela

Who is the driver?

It's only natural, that when you are ready to embark on any interesting journey, you don't want to waste any time; you want to go at speed down the first fast road that appears to be in the direction you want to go!

But this journey is going to be different. Carefully choosing your best route is as important as arriving at your perceived destination.

Using your own devised map and selected mode of transport, and having identified your initial goals, the next step is to take a serious look at the person in charge here, the driver – YOU, and understand exactly where you really are right now.

Some clients see this process, this journey, as going straight from A to B. However, we need to ensure that the place you want to end up and the goals that you currently want to achieve, are right for you and exactly what you desire, otherwise you are wasting your time, effort and energy making this journey in the first place.

Before you drive at speed, in the wrong direction, this is an ideal time to look round and check exactly where you are in relation to where you think you are.

The exercises in this chapter will help you realise where you are physically and mentally in your current life, then in subsequent chapters we will delve deeper to find out all about you as a person, so you can get to know yourself better and then chart an informed course.

It doesn't matter if you've seen yourself as a captain at the helm, a pilot in a plane or plotting a course by foot through the countryside. The person who is charting the course, and that's you, I will refer to as 'the driver'.

If you were setting off on any journey you would expect the driver/pilot to know where they are, in order to be able to navigate and travel safely to the desired destination.

The key thing I have noticed when mentoring, is that most people are unaware and just don't know themselves well enough, nor where they truly are right now.

As this is your own personal journey, it's essential that you know enough about yourself and where your life is now, for you to make informed judgements about the course you need to take - to enable you to create the future you really want.

Chapter Four - Charting your course

To understand yourself, you will need a method of accessing the necessary information. I will explain in simple terms how to get to do that.

We all have ideas about ourselves that we have gained from our particular life experiences. We then express these ideas through our words and actions. Most people aren't aware of how they have processed input from their personality and experience. Somehow, they are not up-to-date with where they are right now in the present, and not as in touch with their real thoughts and ideas as they should be - in effect, they haven't quite caught up with themselves. This is evident when clients are surprised by the results of what they **really** think, as revealed by the exercises.

I have also observed that in more serious cases when people suppress their feelings and do not accept what is going on in their minds, they can become physically or mentally ill because of it.

Lack of not knowing or understanding yourself, ignoring your true feelings and emotions, not acknowledging stress and pressure, and/or having negative thoughts, can cause a vicious cycle, making you feel stuck, or in some cases, resulting in depression or even a breakdown.

If you are experiencing depression, or if you have any physical or mental health problems that requires professional advice or support, you should contact a health practitioner and seek qualified help. Please address these issues, and don't suffer in silence.

Getting to know yourself better has all sorts of advantages, (which we will explore in later chapters), but my consistent experience has been that the more you know and understand yourself, the easier and more successful your journey will be.

Transcending the mind

You are now going to learn how to transcend your mind and in the process, get to know yourself better. To give you a greater understanding of transcending your mind, I will explain the background of my methods of using spontaneous words and the drawing of pictures.

Background of transcending the mind

When I look back, I was quite a privileged child in more ways than one. I had a wonderful family, and friends, lived in a lovely house, with a large garden to play in. We went on marvellous family holidays by the sea, and travelled abroad, something I adored. I didn't have a private education but went to a local school close to home that was known as 'state of the art'. It was a beautiful new school, set on acres of land, and one of the reasons my parents moved into the area.

However, for all this idyllic childhood, and the wonderful new facilities the school had to offer, learning was a nightmare for me as a child, I just hated trying to learn and so school was a place where I didn't achieve. I had no idea how other children knew the answers to questions and understood figures and numbers. I kept the same school reading book for weeks on end; one of my worst struggles was with writing my name.

Then one Christmas, my elder brother, who was a great artist, received a drawing set. He would do a drawing and then run and show Mum. When it came to my turn, instead of trying to create a picture, I took the note pad and drew each of the letters of my name over the whole page - but not in the right order nor in a straight line, as I didn't know how.

When I ran to show Mum what I had drawn, she looked

Chapter Four - Charting your course

closely at it and was obviously thinking about what I had done. Then she said, "Well look at that, you do know the letters of your name, don't you?" She then asked me if I could try and put the letters in the right order and in a straight line. As I didn't know how to do either of those things, I shook my head.

Mum took a ruler and wrote the letters in the right order in a row, so I could only see one word at a time on the paper. Instantly, I could now see the word. Using a ruler I copied the letters in order, again and again, until I got it. I had finally learnt how to spell my name! Next Mum got my school reading book and used a card to cover everything on the page, revealing only one word at a time. I could now start to make sense and learn each word. We progressed to me holding a card under each word to separate them so I only saw one word at a time. In this way, during the school holidays, Mum actually taught me to read.

I returned to school thrilled that I could now read and write and was instantly taken out of the additional remedial class. Can you believe it, the teachers were furious with my parents and accused them of interfering with my learning! At that time, the education authorities appeared not to welcome interference from parents in their child's education and despite the fact that for the first two years at that school their methods hadn't worked for me, they didn't like it that my parents had found a way to help me…

With practice at home in the evenings, within weeks I could read any book a child of my age should be able to read. It was like a miracle.

I continued to have some difficulty with spelling and grammar, my mathematics was poor and every new thing that I started to learn was incredibly difficult for me, but my parents had proved to me that there was always going to be a way for me to be as good as my peers. They just needed to help me identify the problem and together we would find the answer by finding an alternative way to learn. This was a revelation to me.

That Christmas, a simple plain sheet of paper and pen allowed me to transcend what was in my mind - to see a solution to something that I knew was a problem, but couldn't explain.

From then on I always had an exercise book and pen nearby, and by using the page like a mirror to reflect what was in my mind, the problem was copied as a visual image on a page. Seeing it on the page enabled my parents and I to identify and resolve the problem.

You have to know your own mind to identify the problem, before you can go forward, and then you will go forward with speed.

Gradually my mother found many ways of teaching me, and these are some of the things that I developed further and are included in this book.

As I got older, I started interpreting my mind through writing and drawing. What became really interesting was that many other people found it useful, including those without any learning difficulties at all. I couldn't believe it, what a revelation to find out that others didn't really know their own minds either!

As my education continued, I still found the school's teaching methods virtually impossible to learn and almost gave up. I learned in secret at home and to cure my boredom whilst at school, I talked through nearly all my lessons. I started to share the benefits of transcending the mind, and spontaneous words and drawings using a piece of paper and a pencil, with my classmates.

By the time I hit senior school, the education of my peers had developed well and I was now helping them through all sorts of teenage problems, and encouraging them to achieve by getting them to know themselves better and find creative ways to develop themselves, their futures and careers.

Without realising it, I had begun to mentor other people. Most of what I did with them involved writing and drawing spontaneously. Little did I know then that I was in training for my own future work as a mentor.

Although I did not achieve very good qualifications at school, by the time I started college at sixteen I was fortunate that the lecturers identified within days that I had learning difficulties and gave me the help I needed to progress. I then thrived at college and did extremely well in my examinations.

Since then, whether working with those starting out in their career or those at the very top, I have used this same technique of transcending the mind through spontaneous words and drawings.

Everyone has benefited from understanding and getting to know themselves better on paper, through this method. Sometimes this has completely changed people's lives.

Happily, I discovered very recently, that the process of putting thoughts down on paper in words and images, is now no longer considered silly, but recognised as a highly effective tool.

Understanding where you are now

The same method of writing and drawing that my parents used to identify my learning difficulties and allowed me to learn, also helped me to express my feelings and emotions when I was older. It was incredibly useful to learn how to put that down on paper, and will be a valuable tool for you as well.

All the exercises in this book involve transferring facts from your life, from your mind onto paper. We will use this method to help identify where you are right now, by using spontaneous words and drawings.

How to find out where you are right now

I have specialised in interpreting people's words and drawings, and I am fascinated when the images they draw or words they write speak volumes to them. I need to say very little, as they can clearly interpret what they have found out about themselves. In the vast majority of cases individuals understand their own spontaneous words and drawings. On the odd occasion, if people are really stuck, I sometimes interpret for them, until they are able to start interpreting for themselves.

Where are you at the moment?

Transcending your mind through spontaneous words and drawing

For this exercise I want you to find somewhere you can relax, take a few deep breaths, now ask your mind to provide you with five words to describe the way you think and feel, that sums up your life at the moment.

I want you to write down the first five words that come into your mind:

1.   2.   3.   4.   5.

These are the words right at the forefront of your mind; they are your unconscious priorities. What do they say to you? Take a moment and write your responses to these questions, or anything else that comes into your mind.

Chapter Four - Charting your course

Do they surprise you?

Are they positive or negative?

Do any of the words reflect something you have been pondering?

Are they something you want or don't want in your life?

Are they something you need to act upon?

Are you surprised that any of the words reflected something so high on the agenda for you?

Where are you at the moment?

To investigate further, now draw a picture that depicts where you see yourself in your life right now. Again, relax and let your mind flow freely and then draw your picture straight onto the page.

Once you have sketched your picture take some time to look at it and understand it. If you are feeling positive, that may be reflected by an image in your picture, such as a sun in the sky, or a smiling face.

Does your picture show a negative image?

Are you in the picture?

Are your loved ones in the picture?

Does it reflect your hobbies or interests?

Is it work-related ?

Whatever you have drawn it is personal to you, and may have meaning only for you.

Most people can interpret their own drawings straight away, for others it may not appear to have any relevance or reveal anything of importance. Don't worry, experience has shown me that different exercises have varying results and/or benefits. Simply continue.

This is an exercise that is useful when you want to gain some clarity on your thinking at any point, particularly if you are in a confused or unhappy state.

Let's now look at some interpreted drawings

Chapter Four - Charting your course

Learn to interpret your drawings

Here are some sample drawings, and an interpretation of each.

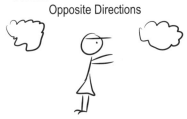
Opposite Directions

This woman had difficulty knowing where to go next in her life. As you look at this drawing you will notice that the head and the feet are going in opposite directions. As soon as I pointed this out to her she recognised that this was a reflection of her life, which she did feel was going in two directions. After some discussion, it was revealed that she had two men in her life and had to make a life-changing decision.

Man in Train

This drawing was done by a client when asked to draw an image of a train on a track. The instruction was to include everyone in his life and to let the drawing encompass every aspect of how he lived. Someone with a strong sense of self drew this picture, and as you can see, the only person he really considered was himself. The man didn't see things holistically - he was at the centre of his own world.

This person had failed at managing people in two jobs, but was desperate to be a successful manager. We discussed the drawing and he identified with what he saw and understood from his picture (so apparently did his family when the picture was shown to them later) that he was totally self-centred. The drawing helped identify a problem. The next step was for this man to then review all aspects of his life, including those in his job. Added to this was some good management training. This client then implemented the strategy in his workplace and is now a highly successful manager.

Chapter Four - Charting your course

Cross on a page

This is what one client drew when I asked him to do a picture of his map and the transport he had chosen for the start of his journey. He just drew a cross on a page, and then looked away. I have seen people draw a cross often.

I asked what this represented, and he told me that the picture depicted his life: a big negative cross. He was shocked at what he had drawn, and the realisation that he hated his life.

But that cross started him on a wonderful journey. He was finally ready to face the challenge of finding out what he could do to improve his life. Just a week later, he drew a much more positive picture, of a plane taking off, and he then continued on this new journey. He didn't actually change his job or personal circumstances, but he improved every area of his current life and took up his life-long ambition of learning to be a glider pilot.

This drawing illustrates an empty boat. A woman in senior management drew it. When asked to explain the picture, she said, "I'm going aimlessly nowhere." I asked her to give me five spontaneous words. Interestingly they were: *empty life, empty purse, empty house, empty head, empty heart*. She was surprised by both her visual images and words.

Empty Boat

I then worked with her to fill the emptiness of her life, which eventually became very full, including getting a new job, the experience of which gave her great pleasure.

Chapter Four - Charting your course

The Entrepeneur

Entrepreneurs usually draw in the centre of the page, often it is just one object, with no people present. Their images usually show great energy, which accurately reflects entrepreneurs, as they are generally very energetic. Their pictures often show an object going in a positive direction, either heading upwards or going from side to side on the page.

Evolving

In the course of my working life, I have witnessed some clients who don't want to evolve in their lives, because this means sacrificing characteristics and attitudes that they don't feel they can change about themselves. Sometimes they have become stuck because of this. They feel they won't have so much fun anymore if they change. But this is not the case. You can progress, mature and move on and still retain your positive experiences or characteristics of youth.

I feel it's a shame that society has introduced labels for different age groups. From what I have observed where I live, if you're classed as an adolescent you may well be thought off as irresponsible; if you're an old-aged pensioner then you may be thought of as past it. It seems nonsense to think of individuals this way.

I have a completely different way of thinking that I would like to share with you. I believe that we are all a unique blend of attitudes of mind. I know many adolescents that are more responsible than some adults, and some retirees who are more active than youngsters.

And when it comes to the term "middle-aged" how on earth

are we all going to know when the phase of our middle age is? The day we leave the planet and halve the number of years we have had?! Therefore, my view is:

Your mental age isn't calculated by counting the years that you have lived, but your attitude of mind.

We are all changing all of the time. Don't fear evolving. We all need to be constantly moving forward so we don't get stuck in a rut.

Next are some exercises to see how you have evolved, and then you will view your current attitude of mind. Finally, complete the exercises which will help clarify where you want to go in your life.

It is important for you to understand evolving, because in the course of this and your life-long journey, you will need to accept that on some occasions you will have to re-assess your original plan or goal in order to evolve and develop further.

We are going to see exactly how you have personally evolved through previous goal setting. We are all growing and developing all of the time; layers, or stages of your life have shaped and formed you into the person you are today. The answers to how you have evolved all dwell in your unique memory.

Note: If during this exercise you come across some past experience that becomes a problem for you and is adversely affecting your life today, I would ask you to seriously consider bringing in someone else to travel on this part of your journey with you, such as a health practitioner or a professional in the relevant area, who can help and support you.

Looking at your life in evolving layers

I want you to go back in time, looking over your life, and start to imagine what your thoughts were at different ages. I have suggested some ages below, but of course you can choose whatever is suitable for you.

You will, in effect, be using your memory to discover what your goals and aims were in the past, and how you may have changed and altered your opinions over time. This will let you see how you evolved from then to where you are now, which will enable you to move onto what you want these results to look like in your future.

The aim of this exercise is to demonstrate your ability to change.

Evolving from when you were a child

Imagine yourself aged eight – or any childhood age you prefer.

Just close your eyes and go back in your memory, and remember yourself again as a child.

What did you look like? What did you like to eat? Who were your friends? What were your dreams and ambitions?

Now write five words that sum up your priorities and ambitions at that age.

1   2   3   4   5

When you have done that, I want you to come back to yourself as you are now. Then see you and your younger self meeting and having a conversation. Imagine saying what you would say to that child. If they are frightened, re-assure them. If they wonder what life has in store in the future, tell them. If they have made mistakes, forgive them. Tell them all that you have achieved in life.

Evolving from when you were a child

Write your thoughts in the space below

Imagine yourself aged thirteen - or another teenage year

You are now going to repeat the process you just did, but from the perspective of when you were thirteen, or your chosen age. Use your imagination to remember when you were that age. What did you wear? What ambitions did you have? What did you perceive as problems at that time?

Now write five words that come to you spontaneously, which sum up your priorities and ambitions when you were

Chapter Four - Charting your course

aged thirteen, or your chosen age.

1   2   3   4   5

Now again you are going to imagine and then write a conversation between you, as you are now, and your teenage self. You will probably notice a great difference between the young child and the teenager, but just write down below what you would say. If the teenager is unsure of themselves, re-assure them. What would you as that teenager have wondered about the world that wasn't even in your mind as a young child? If they (you) have made mistakes, had a bad attitude, or did something wrong, then forgive them.

Evolving from when you were a teenager

Write your thoughts in the space below

Your evolving future

The journey that you are taking now is related to your future.

Now that you have evolved from child to adolescent, and then to an adult, the next step is to consider how you want to evolve now and in the future, and what characteristics and attitudes you wish to retain or develop.

Write down what would sum up your top priorities and ambitions for your future.

Write your thoughts in the space below

Chapter Four - Charting your course

An experience of evolving

I work with a world-famous university, and one of my students, after years of study had just qualified as a doctor. She came to me because she was deeply unhappy and wanted desperately to discuss her future with me. I thought she would be a fine doctor, but there was just one problem: she had loved studying but hated the actual job.

She worked on getting to know herself and we spent a lot of time identifying problems and talking through what she wanted from her career. We discussed many options; including her remaining as a doctor but at another hospital, or looking at a different career in medicine, such as becoming a family doctor, or going into research. Although we kept seeking new options within the same field, nothing seemed to satisfy her.

When we did the exercise on evolving, her answers from when she was a child were very illuminating. All her responses were on the same theme: Mother wants me to be a doctor, Father wants me to be a doctor, the family wants me to be a doctor, and my teachers think I should be a doctor. Her own thought at that age was simple: I don't want to be a doctor.

Her picture was a cross in the centre of the page. She explained that her parents were both in medicine and had been devastated when her sibling had decided to go into another profession. So she had gone into medicine to please them. Her young child, in the 'conversation' she had as part of the exercise, told her that she had wanted to work in journalism, or press and public relations. "I don't care what I have to do to get there, that's what I want to do," was her response. She remembered that as a child she used to create magazines, and write articles for them, and that was what satisfied her the most.

I asked her why, since she felt so strongly about not

becoming a doctor, did she not address this sooner? Basically, she had procrastinated until the moment of being qualified and starting a job in medicine. Sadly, she had just suppressed her feelings until finally she couldn't do it any more.

The irony is that when she eventually told her parents, they had no problem in her changing careers. They knew that their other child had made the right decision in not going into the medical profession and they had supported their daughter in going into medicine because they believed that it was what she wanted to do. Her parents had, over time, evolved and become more liberal - but they hadn't shared their new attitude with their daughter. This meant that she had spent years qualifying for a profession she didn't want to enter into, and actually need not have done so.

However, very soon after our work together she went into public relations and publishing, which she adores. No doubt she has been selected to be the first aid person in her company, so no experience is wasted!

My experience is that negative habits or modes of behaviour can pass from one generation to the next - without individuals ever questioning them, or communicating their real thoughts and feelings about them. However, through effort, I have seen these cycles alter, and new useful, healthy patterns emerge.

Chapter Four - Charting your course

Progress Report:

You are making good progress by:

- ❏ *understanding exactly where you are in life*
- ❏ *being better informed to chart your course*
- ❏ *understanding the benefits of transcending your mind*
- ❏ *learning how to interpret your drawings*
- ❏ *seeing how you can evolve and retain the characteristics and attitudes about yourself you like*
- ❏ *learning how you have evolved and how you can continue in the future*

Do you want to chart any progress to your original map or create a new map to explain where you are? (Optional)

Having completed this chapter are there any notes you wish to enter in your note book?

Chapter Four - Charting your course

Chapter Five - Changing position

Chapter 5

Changing position

"Whether you believe you can, or you believe you can't, you're right either way."
- Henry Ford

My own experience is that the start of a journey is exciting, the middle bit can be difficult at times, and the arrival/achieving is wonderful! As you travel, treasure each successful moment, and whenever difficult challenges lie ahead, just focus on the finishing-line and how good you will feel when you get there.

In this chapter we are going to increase the pace of your journey and make even more positive progress along your charted course. To do this we are now going to review and develop your goals, build strategies and focus on

Chapter Five - Changing position

implementing them. You can accelerate the process by using your own Personal Development Charts as you go along.

So let's review your Initial Goals List. By now you may be ready to add to the list, or alter your priorities. Afterwards, these goals will be transferred onto a Personal Development Chart. You can then increase your motivation to achieve your goals, or speed up, by creating a Personal Development Tracking Chart

If you want additional charts, visit The Achiever's Journey website www.theachieversjourney.com and click on 'Chart Templates'. **Example - Personal Development Chart**

Example - Personal Development Chart

This chart will show how to list your goals. I have provided several different goals to show you varying areas that you might want to work with. I suggest you choose how many you want to work on at any one time, and be realistic. It's better to achieve one goal successfully, than struggle with five.

Example - Personal Development Chart

Status	Goals	Strategies for Implementing Goals	Goals Implemented
Short term	Get a new job	Prepare and update my CV Buy newspapers and magazines with job vacancies Identify competitors for vacancies Search Internet for vacancies	Yes Yes No Yes
Short term	Stop smoking	Cut down by 1 cigarette a day Increase time between cigarettes Stop going outside at work with smokers Put up the poster of smoker's-damaged lung	Yes Yes now 3 hours Yes Yes
Medium term	Change my car	Start looking for a car in the: Newspaper Car magazines Sell existing car online Car dealerships Ask Mark if he is selling his car because it would be ideal	Ordered subscription Yes Awaiting details Look at Weekends
Medium term	Exercise	Join gym Start walking to work Get my bike out again Ask Jane to come walking with me on Sundays	
Long term	Start to learn French	Purchase CD for the car Go on holiday to France next year	

My Personal Development Chart

Status (Short, medium or long term)	Goals	Strategies for Implementing Goals (What are you going to actually do to make these goals happen)	Goals Implemented

Chapter Five - Changing position

Now that you have worked out what you want to achieve and what you need to do to get there, you may want to move on to creating your Personal Development Tracking Chart.

Personal Development Tracking Chart

This has two purposes: firstly, to record your progress, and secondly, to be used as a long-term visual record to motivate yourself. A visual record is a simple and effective way to keep track of your progress.

Here is an example of how to fill in the chart. My examples are just suggestions, as only you can judge how much you can realistically achieve, and in what time frame. You may choose to track daily, weekly, or even monthly, depending on what time scale you have set up for your goals. You can include short, medium, and long-term goals in your Personal Development Tracking Chart, or just the short-term goals you want to achieve. It's as flexible as you want it to be.

(When filling out this chart think how good you are going to feel when you have achieved these goals)

Chapter Five - Changing position

Example - Personal Development Tracking Chart

No.	Goals	Week 1 (Day, week or month)	Week 2	Week 3	Week 4	Week 5	Totals and Comments
1.	Get a new job in another firm	Prepare CV	Send CV, continue to look for vacancies	1st interview	2nd interview	Another interview	Interviews going well
2.	Reduce my Smoking from 31 cigs a day	30 cigarettes per day	29 cigarettes per day	28 cigarettes per day	27 cigarettes per day	26 cigarettes per day	Since new initiative I feel better, more in control. This long term way of quitting is working for me.
3.	Change my car	Work out how to finance new car	Prepare old car for sale - valuation	Looked at cars for idea of market	I have identified exact car I want	Ask for part exchange deal	Realised that if I shop around I will get a better deal. Aim to purchase in six weeks time.
4.	Exercise at gym 2 hours / week	Average 3 x 1hr gym Walked to work	Got cold - no fitness this week	Average 1 x 1hr gym Walked to work	Average 3 x 1hr gym Walked to work	Average 3 x 1hr gym Walked to work	Achieved goal - will continue with gym and exercise
5.	Learn to speak French	Looked into classes	Bought French CD - use on way to work	Joined French class + CD	Continued French class + CD	Continued French class + CD	Progressing well - now on Stage 2 verbal French course, booked holiday to France.

Chapter Five - Changing position

Personal Development Tracking Chart

No.	Goals	Date Day, week or month					Totals and comments

Chapter Five - Changing position

What you will notice about the results

I suggest that as you fill in these charts you add up the totals/results every once in a while. If you are doing results daily, try totalling them up at the end of the week. You may find your efforts will be greater as you head towards the result day! Great, that's motivation!

Don't expect your achievements to progress at the same rate all the time, because chances are they won't. We all have better days than others, and though sometimes you will take two steps forward and one step back, just remember, all the time you are still moving forward and achieving.

Chapter Five - Changing position

DO YOU WANT TO CHANGE YOUR CAREER OR LOOK FOR A NEW JOB?

If YES read on

If NO then move on to Chapter 6

Changing Career or Getting a New Job

A lot of my clients do the Achiever's Journey when they are looking to make a major change in direction in their lives, such as changing their career or job.

I have considerable experience in this field, as I was a joint owner of a highly successful recruitment agency, handling various salary levels. Latterly I specialised in employing very senior personnel.

Much of my mentoring is for a change in career, improving performance or gaining a promotion. Therefore, in this chapter I have provided some useful information about looking for a new employment position, either salaried or voluntary.

Preparation

It is vital that you invest enough time and effort in preparation for a change in career or job.

I have worked with several clients who were disillusioned after making a solid decision to create a major change in their career, and then not seeing any progress. After a few months they may have had a couple of interviews, but didn't get past stage one, so they turned to me for mentoring help and motivation. When I ask what preparation they had done, the answer was more often than not, very little.

Common 'Reasons' for Non-Progress

Do any of these sound familiar?

1. **There just aren't the jobs around.**
2. **I applied for jobs and never heard back.**
3. **Only got to first interview stage and can't understand why I didn't get any further.**

Are you feeling stuck, anxious or depressed about your current situation? Don't worry, help is at hand!

If you really want this change to happen, then it will. You can do it, you just need to want it enough. To give yourself the best chance, you must spend enough time preparing yourself. Getting promoted, changing jobs or starting a new career is both a major challenge and lifestyle change, so give it the time and respect it deserves.

Reality Check

It's my firm belief that you must always be positive, based on reality. It is very important that you start with a reality check because it can help you improve yourself and your situation.

But, you cannot change the world, or how other people behave. Life often isn't fair, and when you are making lifestyle choices, the unfairness seems to be at its peak. Bear the following in mind:

1. **You will need to allocate time to prepare if you wish to move forward.**
2. **Your Curriculum Vitae (CV) may seem to take ages to put together, but it helps if you constantly keep it updated.**
3. **You will more than likely get disappointed and disillusioned at some point along the way.**

Chapter Five - Changing position

Don't let this get to you. Simply say to yourself, "Right, next!" If you hit disappointment just pick yourself up, brush yourself down and carry on. Press onwards and upwards and don't look back.

4. Not all employers will acknowledge your job application and letter.

The disappointment of not receiving responses can be one of the biggest factors in getting depressed when looking for a new job. However, often a potential employer has hundreds of CV's to look at and sometimes has to delay the interviewing process for one reason or another. Additionally, some employers make it a point only to respond once someone has been appointed.

So accept that there may be many reasons why you haven't heard back and please don't let this affect you.

Even after interviews, you won't always get a letter from employers to let you know whether you got the job or not. If you haven't heard from them after a couple of weeks, it is perfectly okay to contact the company again to enquire about the outcome. This lets them know you are seriously interested as well as getting the results of the interview.

If you don't get the job you applied for, there may be others coming up, and the fact that you took the time to contact them again may weigh in your favour, so ask to remain on file for any other similar positions that may come up. Additionally, you can ask if they have any colleagues in business who might benefit from the experience and skills you have to offer.

Updating CV, References, and Portfolio

I often get asked what a Curriculum Vitae (CV) should contain. The answer is simple. I want to see a concise CV that informs me in a reasonable amount of space, of all relevant details about you to allow me to decide whether you are suitable for the position.

Your CV is often used by an assessor to make a decision on whether to invite you for a first round interview, or keep you on company files for the future.

Length of CV is another thing that worries people, but I have received equally correct CV's on two sheets of paper and five, depending on the vacancy. It's not the number of pages but the relevance of the information it contains that matters.

Include all Relevant Information

Details of your work experience are vital to the employer assessing your suitability for the post you have applied for, and not just from your current work history.

Sample CV format:

What employers request by way of information about prospective employees has altered significantly in the past few years. Different countries also have different rules of protocol about what is asked.

Obviously, the information you provide on your CV is your decision, However, a potential employer may also request further information from you.

Below is an example of what potential employers generally want to see included in a CV. And remember to always send a covering letter informing the prospective employer why you think you are right for the position. If you would like more help with your CV, there are many excellent books on the subject or you may wish to look on the Internet.

CV

Name: Millie Westey

Date of birth: 10/12/84 (optional)

Full address:
Charlecote House
Seafield Road
Lavenham
England BB21 3AT

Full Contact Details:
Phone daytime:
Phone evenings:
Phone mobile:
Fax:
Email: anyone@anyinternet.com

Preferred contact option: mobile or Email

Nationality: British/Chinese (optional)

Marital Status: (optional**)**

Overview of Career To-Date

Right at the top give an overview of your relevant information, no more than two paragraphs. For example, An entrepreneurial manager with ten years experience in blue chip companies ...

Previous positions

(List in descending date order from your current position)

....

Qualifications

....

Personal Interests

List your current interests

References

A lot of potential employers ask you not to send references before you are offered the job, but I'll let you into a secret. When I have been selecting people for interviews, I certainly read them and I know many other selectors do the same. It can give a candidate an edge if their references are good, and relevant, so you might want to include them.

Update your work portfolio

If you are a writer, graphic artist, photographer or similar, potential employers will require samples of your work – often a history of your achievements, as well as your most recent work

Covering letter

As an assessor, I like to see a covering letter with a CV. It gives you a chance to explain things and put over your good points, and if well crafted, will create some rapport with your potential employer. I know people who have gone straight through to interviews on the content of their covering letter. So remember to give yourself the edge by always including one with your CV.

Now you have completed your covering letter and CV let's look at the next stage, the interview.

Preparing for an interview

You never get a second chance to make a good first impression ...

Once you are successful and get an interview, the preparation needs to be stepped up a gear. I have devised a checklist for you to work through, but before you begin this process I would also like you to think through and plan for the financial implications connected to the career move you wish to make. Changing your lifestyle or career will inevitably make a difference to many aspects of your life, so just make sure you include them in this process. This way you will be prepared if questions come up in the interview about salary, willingness to relocate, and so on.

Chapter Five - Changing position

1   Research

The first and most essential step is to research the potential employer. What can you find out about the company? Check on their background, market position and products. Look at their website as you can often find valuable information there, particularly if they list press releases on latest developments in the company and its subsidiaries.

2   Date and time

Even if you have written confirmation of an interview, always ring to confirm, the day before the appointment. Ask to speak to the interviewer – they will be impressed – and you will have registered your presence with them before you meet.

3   Interview location

Don't think that you know where your interview is taking place, make sure you know exactly where you are going, and also how long it will take you to get there. Get an area map, check on the Internet or ring the company's switchboard and ask for specific directions, or a map; some organisations also create maps to send out to clients and new employees.

It doesn't bode well when I have someone ring up for an interview, with ten minutes to the allotted time, and they are lost. Carefully check your route before leaving and give yourself plenty of time. And if you have an important interview, and live in the area, try travelling there on a trial run before the date of the appointment.

4 Prepare the night before

Life is full of last-minute delays; so don't leave everything to the morning of the interview. It will pay you to prepare the night before and get everything ready that you will need: clothes, briefcase, portfolio, written references, map.

5 Last-minute check

I have had people turn up for an interview with the price tag still on their suit; and others turn up on the wrong day.

6 Switch your mobile phone off

Carrying a mobile phone is second nature for many people, so much so you forget you are carrying it. However, you won't forget it if it rings during your interview. You would be amazed how many people miss this simple check, so do remember to turn your mobile phone off.

My Recruiting Secrets

Having attended interviews, I have never forgotten what it is like to be actively trying to get a job. From the other side, I have selected candidates for interviews for client companies, and also recruited my own staff, so I know how important it is to get the right people. I continually bear all this in mind when dealing with both candidates and potential employers.

I work very hard to keep an open mind when interviewing, but there is a difference between keeping an open mind, not having prejudices, and identifying bad manners and attitude. If you are going to be selected by me this is the main point I would want you to remember:

Everything you do or say, you are judged on.

That is the simple truth. We constantly make opinions and judgements about everyone in our lives. If the delivery man doesn't arrive on time, we judge him on it. If a neighbour or friend buys something new, we often automatically (mentally) admire or criticise their taste.

What you must understand is that from the time you first make any contact with a potential employer you are going to be judged. It's a bit like a first date; you are interested and want to find out all about the person. You observe their behaviour, voice, mannerisms, manners and how they present themselves. A potential employer is always doing exactly the same with you.

Viewing retirement in a positive way

Although we have been focusing on change in employment, for many people the major change that they are facing is retirement. Happily, this has changed so much these days and it can be whatever you want it to be.

If you are among those anticipating retirement, before it happens is the best time to make a plan. This should include financial planning plus whatever activities and hobbies or even a job you might want to take up. Working whilst retired is now often seen these days an extension of your career or working life.

Whatever you want to do it's best to be prepared and plan for it.

Chapter Five - Changing position

Progress Report

You are well into the journey now. You have:

- ❏ *created and understood the importance of a Personal Development Chart*
- ❏ *had the opportunity of completing your Personal Development Chart.*
- ❏ *travelled further by completing your Personal Development Tracking Chart to record your progress in achieving your goals.*
- ❏ *taken active steps by turning your goals into achievements*
- ❏ *the know-how to prepare yourself for this exciting challenge, if one of your goals is to change your career or job.*
- ❏ *vital information about your curriculum vitae, references and portfolio*
- ❏ *seen how retirement can be viewed positively*

At this point you might want to:

- *change your mode of transport*
- *chart your progress on your existing map: visualise where you are on this journey*
- *add comments to your notebook*

You can either take a rest now or press on with the journey. As with all journeys, don't continue driving if you're tired, take a break.

Chapter Five - Changing position

Chapter Six - Making Good Progress 87

Chapter 6

Making Good Progress

The pessimist sees the difficulty in every opportunity.
The optimist sees the opportunity in every difficulty.
                                    - Sir Leonard Winston Churchill

Don't let obstacles get in your way

My experience is that some people who want to go forward with their lives, often want change and improvements, but they don't want to make any effort. It is as if they believe there is a magic wand that will make positive changes happen instantly. However, once they overcome this, and make even the smallest of effort, things gradually gain momentum and they start to move in the direction they wish to go.

With the right preparation you have now made great progress, covered a lot of ground, on track and heading in the right direction to achieve your goals. Now that you are making such good progress, we need to ensure that you are not slowed down or diverted by any obstacles.

I want to share with you some of the most beneficial techniques I personally utilise, that you may wish to implement into your everyday routine, for an easier journey and greater piece of mind.

To implement your chosen goals, you need to keep yourself motivated to keep moving forward, but also be aware of anything that might hold you back.

Note: Remember if you have any physical or mental health issues that have not been addressed, or are struggling mentally to cope, please seek professional support, before continuing on.

Using Improved Software for your Mind

I will not give a scientific explanation of this process, but will simply explain how you can start to think in more effective ways.

These tried-and-tested methods work — if you choose to work at consciously using them.

Imagine your mind is like a computer, and you have a chance to install in this computer a wonderful new software programme, one that allows you to have total control over all forms of communication, (both incoming and outgoing), and how it affects you.

Would you like more control over which communications are allowed entry and which are blocked, (similar to a (100%) virus scanner/blocker), to help you deal with your emotions, and life situations better?

If you have the time and the inclination, you might want to

Chapter Six - Making Good Progress

look at producing your own new ways of thinking – your own improved software. But to save you some time, here are some ideas that have worked for others in the past, for you to test-drive.

My (imaginary) software works 24/7. You are always in charge, automatically (consciously) accepting and filing positive, helpful data, or rejecting/deflecting unwanted communications or information.

This software has two channels for receiving: internal and external.

Internal communication –

Your own thoughts.

External communication –

What you take in from outside yourself, in whatever form that might take, visual / verbal: the written word or drawings, speech, music, body language etc.

We all receive and deal with thousands of communications at once, and naturally aren't aware of how quickly we process them. But it is not a good idea to keep filling your Inbox with thousands of internal and external communications, and not deal with them properly. Each needs to be assessed, before being rejected or filed.

When a new communication arrives in my Inbox I tend to deal with it immediately, and after consideration, reject it, send it to 'Pending', 'Active', or 'Archive' files. Your files can be anything you choose.

If on the rare occasions I feel overburdened and can't deal with my Inbox straight away, I just take care of the high priorities. At this time I group things into large sections in my inbox and properly file them when I am in the right frame of mind to deal with each issue.

Archive filing

Live files are those we are actively dealing with, and also include our achievements. Archived files are the old files we have stored away, most we are probably aware of, but not all. We have archived files in our mind that we have collected over the years; some of these will be valuable, other files may be not very useful – and in effect, 'excess baggage'.

Some of your archived files will be happy memories, which are nice to re-visit. But if you need to deal with an archive that is hindering your progress, and feel you cannot do it on your own, you may need assistance from a professional. Don't let this be an obstacle. If you can't deal with difficult files/memories by yourself, get the right help and support.

Understanding positive and negative energy

Simply put, I see all life experience as either positive or negative energy. For most of us, positive thoughts make us feel happy, and negative thoughts cause us to feel unhappy.

Gaining and retaining positive energy

Physical-related things, like a healthy diet, exercise, having a good balance in our lives, and taking care of ourselves, can make us feel great.

We get energy from the sun or from the earth beneath our feet, and also by creating happy living and working environments.

We also benefit from taking care of our mental health and energy. Achieving goals is a great boost to our energy and mental health.

Chapter Six - Making Good Progress

When you receive a compliment, allow that positive energy up into your forehead, to fill it with light, ready for your mind to allow it into your brain Inbox. The positive energy you have received will then be stored in the relevant file in your mind, and become another resource to make you feel good.

Remember to write down positive thoughts, experiences, or achievements, and place them where you can regularly see them. Re-visiting these positive comments or events has an energising effect, which will further brighten the golden light in your brain.

If you receive constructive criticism, take it to your forehead and consider it, before allowing it into the Inbox. If it is relevant or helpful, the Inbox can safely file it under 'Lessons learned' and learn from it. When you allow it through it will go in as a positive thought, and create more light.

Deflecting negative energy

If you think that someone is sending negative energy to you, hoping to deflate you, this is how you can handle it. When the communication reaches you, imagine that negative energy landing at your feet, far away from your mind and its precious Inbox.

Now you are better able to assess the communication, to determine whether it is constructive criticism meant to actually help you, or whether it is deliberately there to deflate you. If you think this is the case then you have full control to carefully deal with the situation, changing the negative energy into positive. File and deal with the matter appropriately, then the negative energy has not affected or harmed you.

In some cases you may wish to return it to its source, to the person who sent it, by saying silently in your mind "return".

It will then instantly return, via the route it first travelled, back to the mind that sent it.

A word of warning: you must not, for any reason, return anger or feelings of revenge, because that would be giving your own precious power away. Just simply think "return" and smile, because you have just won; the negative energy has been deflected. Additionally, the person who sent the negative energy has just given some of their own power away to you. So you can relax, knowing this negative energy was not allowed into your mind.

If it is a more serious matter then imagine keeping the negative energy in your foot, out of harms way, until you have made an informed decision. At times you may feel it is appropriate to seek professional advice before you make this decision.

Just imagine, if a nasty person had their negative energy on a "return to sender" basis every time they sent a nasty thought, they would soon be drowning in their own negative energy. I do believe that what goes around comes around.

You can allow each communication to go no further than the forehead, before being assessed. So any challenging communications go no further than your feet, prior to evaluation.

Overcoming obstacles

We are going to look at the most common obstacles that you might come across and have to deal with on your journey.

Not allowing fear to get in your way

When working on implementing your goals, whatever you do, try not to let any fear get in your way.

Chapter Six - Making Good Progress

Most people have fears; life can be frightening at times. We need to have some ingrained fears, to prevent us from walking in front of oncoming traffic or placing our hands in a burning fire...

Fear is to do with fight or flight. If you were a little bird and saw a cat trying to pounce on you, you would move quickly, wouldn't you? The chemical reaction and the brain activity of this little bird would say, "It's time for me to fight or take flight". The bird would have little chance to fight as it is too small. Therefore it would choose to fly away.

We can put fear into ourselves by our own faulty thinking; this unrealistic fear isn't helpful.

Unrealistic fears can have consequences in your life, so you need to address these as soon as you can.

If any self doubts or fears are troubling you, or preventing you from moving forward, it is a good idea to talk to friends or family or seek professional help to understand and then eliminate these from your life.

If you do need professional input from others, put them in the passenger seat of your vehicle (or allow them to walk with you) and you will have yet another means of support for the journey.

Dealing with anger

Most of us get angry at times, but often it is a wasted emotion. If someone has wronged you, take early action to address it, or use a method for not letting it bother you, like the Improved Mind Software.

If someone's words or actions make you feel angry and upset, you are giving your power away to that person.

Do you choose to put your energy into healthy, positive things that will grow?

Or are you allowing anger and other negative energies to reduce your positive energy?

Don't let anger get the better of you. I have had to forgive many people in my life for the awful things they have done to me. Forgiveness is an extremely difficult thing, but if you can forgive, it frees you.

Dealing with bullying

Most of us have been bullied at some point, and it is both awful and disgraceful. Unfortunately, bullies look just like other people. They aren't green or blue, they often look like nice people, but bullies have two sorts of people in their lives: those they leave alone and those they choose to bully.

Bullying is totally unacceptable and I have met a lot of people in my career who have been on the receiving end of bullying; each time it saddens me greatly. Bullying has to be addressed early and you must seek proper help.

To address bullying, share what is going on with someone whom you trust. Then together you can seek further advice if necessary from a professional, and create a plan of action to tackle the problem.

Dealing with feeling stuck

We all feel stuck at some time in our lives, just not knowing where to turn next. This is actually a good place to be, because to change things and become unstuck, you have to make a defining move. A decision. It's a bit like being at the front of a queue in a car park, waiting for a space. It's your turn next, but where is the free space? You're not going to find the space sitting where you are, are you? You have to get into first gear and go look for it.

If you feel stuck, move, do something.

Keep looking forwards not sideways nor down. Once you

Chapter Six - Making Good Progress

start to think that everything will go wrong, you can start to actually attract obstacles or problems into your life. We all have things go wrong, but there are ways to deal with them.

Dealing with stress and pressure

We all know how it feels to be under pressure. It is not just other people who put us under pressure; we also create this for ourselves.

Imagine if today, for whatever reason, you weren't able to fulfil all your commitments or responsibilities. Someone else would have to stand in, wouldn't they? Try to delegate as much as you can; you don't have to do it all, all of the time.

If you have pressures from work, talk to someone about the situation, or if necessary, perhaps change your job. Do something about the situation before a real problem arises.

If you have financial issues that are causing you pressure, seek advice. The Citizen's Advice Bureau is very useful, also debt consolidation services. Check telephone or business directories, search the Internet, or get recommendations from friends or colleagues.

At times, we all have pressures, in every aspect of our lives. Work puts us under pressure, also driving, and handling difficult phone calls or conversations. Our loved ones put us under pressure, sometimes without even realising it and I'm sure we all do it to others in our lives.

Some pressures come from unexpected circumstances. These can be difficult situations to deal with because we can't anticipate or pre-empt them.

To handle pressure and stress in our lives, we need to recognise our own limitations and find different ways to cope better.

The answer to dealing with pressure is to actively deal with the situation early on and not to pretend it doesn't exist.

Dealing with depression

No one can make you feel inferior without your consent.
-Eleanor Roosevelt

Depression is awful, I know, because I've experienced it.

Most of the people I come across every day have experienced depression at some point, from those starting off with their career to those who are at the top. I am amazed to the extent that people suffer from it.

Sometimes its hard to identify this condition, so the first thing is to get a professional to give a diagnosis, and then if necessary, help you to find ways to overcome it.

Lots of people get depressed for lots of different reasons. You are not on your own, so don't be too embarrassed to ask for help. There is no need to suffer in silence. Don't just continue to spiral downwards or let the hole get bigger; talk to your doctor, family, friends or counsellor.

The way out of depression is different for everyone, you just need to find the right way for you. Don't get disillusioned if you don't get results immediately or through your first chosen solution. There will be an answer for you. Happily, I have seen many people with serious depression make great recoveries. It may take time. But don't give up!

Chapter Six - Making Good Progress

Recovering from illness

It is especially difficult getting back to your normal life after an extended illness.

Be realistic and plan your return in stages. Go back to work for so many hours at a time, and slowly build up the hours again. Be governed by your doctor's advice. Talk to your employers and colleagues, and explain that you will need time to get back up to speed.

An easy trap to fall into when you are starting to feel better after being off work for an extended period is to think that you can cope with work again straight away. However the pace when you return to work is probably going to be more demanding than you realise.

Nearly three years ago I had three awful operations within six months: surgery on both legs. The second operation should have been a straightforward procedure, but sadly I needed more surgery to remove a large blood clot. I was left with a nasty wound and felt very ill. It took months of healing and rehabilitation to fully resume my mobility and lifestyle. On top of that, only a month after all the surgery, I lost someone very close to me in a dreadful tragedy; the incident left me with horrendous nightmares for months.

It was a terrible time in my life, but I was blessed with a wonderful surgeon and doctor, which helped enormously. However, I was on endless drugs, including morphine to cope with unbearable pain. I lost my energy, concentration, self esteem, and general well-being. The endless months of recuperation left me feeling depressed, frustrated, and outside normal society. I found trying to concentrate very difficult and my normal hectic lifestyle went down to a very slow pace.

The only solution was to look forwards, never sideways or down.

Chapter Six - Making Good Progress

Immediately upon coming out of hospital, after my third operation, I went on a cruise. I had to get onto the ship in a wheelchair, as I couldn't stand up, with my husband carrying a suitcase full of bandages, morphine and other drugs. Ten days later I came off the ship walking and feeling I had the strength to carry on.

With two steps forward and one back, sometimes wondering if I would ever fully recover, it took me the best part of two years to fully recover, from both the physical challenges and emotional events. Gradually, I started exercising with a fitness trainer, went back to work, and moved forward at a pace that was realistic for me and my body. Getting back to work and the fitness programme were the best things I could have done.

On the upside, recovering from the operations gave me time to write this book.

If you are going through any physical or emotional crises, allow yourself sufficient time to recover and return to a normal life.

Chapter Six - Making Good Progress 99

Dealing with a life crisis

A life crisis can happen at any age. I have encountered many people who have had crises or breakdowns of one type or another.

If you are currently experiencing this, you are one of millions in the same boat. Don't worry, you are not on your own, there is help available. Enlist as much help as you can. Deal with this straight away. The day you deal with it can be the turning point, and the first day of your recovery.

Helping with other people's crises

If you are caring for or trying to support someone else who is experiencing a crisis or illness, you too need to get support from others. Look after yourself well by frequently taking time out from the situation. Don't be a martyr.

Enlist help from:

* *Family and friends*
* *Doctor and/or Counsellors*
* *Support groups or Associations*

Resources/support:

* *Internet*
* *Books,*
* *Video, CD's, DVD's*
* *Magazines*
* *Exercise clubs*
* *Fitness instructor*
* *Television programmes and films*

Grief

I have found dealing with grief one of the most difficult things to come to terms with. To be honest, I still have my moments, even long after losing someone, when I feel very sad and find the situation difficult to deal with. Anniversaries especially catch me out: looking at greeting cards in shops, that I won't be buying for a loved one no longer with me.

The worst thing for me when a loved one passed away was the fact that they were gone, after having once been so close. It felt as if they were further away than the end of the universe.

However, someone who had lost many family members, passed on an exercise that has worked very well for me and others, and I would like to share it with you. No matter what your own beliefs and thoughts are on grief, this simple exercise might give you comfort.

For my own process, I visualise my late parents back in the home they loved so much. I see Dad in his beautifully kept garden tending his organic vegetable plot. Mum is cooking in the kitchen, or watching a Wimbledon tennis match on television, or packing to go on holiday. I imagine my late brother in his favourite house, or jogging along the beautiful tree-lined street that he loved so much.

When you are ready, relax in a comfortable, quiet environment. Then imagine your loved one in a safe place - somewhere that they would want to be, and somewhere you can easily imagine. Take some time to be with them and share whatever you need or wish to at this time.

On special dates or anniversaries, I now put flowers next to a photo of a departed loved one, and think of all the good times we shared together.

Grief can be a difficult process. Share how you feel,

try not to bottle it up. Seek information and advice from professionals, and accept the support of those around you.

I understand what you are going through...

Identifying procrastination

One of the biggest obstacles I find from mentoring is procrastination. Putting off and storing up things that should be dealt with. We all do it. We all procrastinate. We put things off that need addressing in one way or another, because we are frightened, or can't be bothered to allocate the necessary time to deal with problems.

I have seen numerous individuals in senior management who progress well, but then don't nurture themselves nor continue to train in their field and as a consequence they fall behind and get stuck when they reach their level of competence.

One MD/CEO decided to partly retire and was offered an ideal non-executive director position on a part-time basis. He came to me, desperate for help; he had never passed his driving test, never used a computer, and couldn't even use a fax machine. For years everything had been done for him. But now the new position required these skills. He had to go on a crash course, forgive the pun, but he made it. Why he had delayed addressing these issues for years was purely out of procrastination, based on fear of the unknown.

When you procrastinate it is as if you have become stuck in mud. It can have serious implications though, including frustration, anxiety and depression. You will always feel better (and your life will probably be better) when the task or problem you have been procrastinating about has been resolved.

I have devised a Procrastination Improvement Sheet, for

you to fill in. You can also use your exercise book or A4 folder for this.

Clients are sometimes amazed at the results - one had over 200 entries!

Procrastination list

I suggest that you create a list and keep a record, starting today, of all the things you need to do, to avoid procrastinating over things currently needing attention, or to be done in your life.

Record the date and how you are going to implement the action you need to take to resolve the issue(s).

You can't address everything at once, so write down how and when each goal will be achieved.

Example - Procrastination Improvement Sheet

Date	Procrastination	Implementation	Task Completed
28/05/09	Not writing down appointments properly	Buy a new diary on Saturday, fill it in daily	Yes 30/05/09
28/05/09	Visit the dentist for a routine check – over a year since I went	Book appointment today	Yes 3/06/09
28/05/09	Paint fence in garden	Buy paint on Saturday and paint 1 panel per evening for 8 days	Yes Completed
28/05/09	Oil squeaky door hinge	Do it today	Completed today
29/05/09	Upgrade anti-virus software	Look on internet	Completed

Chapter Six - Making Good Progress

Procrastination Improvement Sheet

Date	Procrastination	Implementation	Task Completed

Chapter Six - Making Good Progress

Progress Report:

Well done! In this chapter you have covered a lot of ground and have worked at not allowing any obstacles hinder your excellent progress. You have:

- ❑ ***learnt about using Improved Mind Software for your benefit***
- ❑ ***learnt about positive and negative energy and how to deal with it***
- ❑ ***learnt how not to let obstacles get in your way***
- ❑ ***looked at identifying and dealing with fear, anger, bullying, feeling stuck, depression, stress, pressure and grief***
- ❑ ***started to address the things you procrastinate about, using your Procrastination Improvement Sheet***

You have travelled quite a distance now, do you want to chart your progress on your map?

Having completed this chapter are there any notes you wish to enter in your note book?

Now that you know yourself better, you are better informed and able to chart your course more successfully and not let obstacles get in your way. Clients always find this is time well spent during the journey to achieving.

Chapter Seven

Being Organised

I find the harder I work, the more luck I seem to have.
-Thomas Jefferson

You have now made good progress, to ensure that you keep up this good pace and stay on course in the future, you need to fully organise things now. At this stage in your journey I will give you some basic ideas and exercises to achieve this.

The good news is, once you have organised yourself you just need to keep following through. Then not only will you feel so much better, those around you will benefit as well.

How do you currently organise your life?

Let's think about it.

Would being organised make your life easier?

Are you completely or partially organised, in all aspects of your life?

Is your life structured in any way?

When was the last time you identified what needs to be organised in your life? What time do you allocate to planning and implementing disciplines, good habits and systems?

Is your life (and others') affected by your lack of organisation?

Basic organising

Naturally we have to start off by identifying the problem areas - where you aren't organised. We do this by reviewing different sectors of your life. I have provided a basic list of sectors, which you will probably wish to add to. Once you have identified the problems this information is transferred onto a Tracking Chart, to help you implement the steps to reaching your goals.

Sectors of your life for reviewing

Listed below are some possible areas for improvement in your life. Where applicable, add them to your chart. Then add your own.

Personal

Time Organisation: keep day planner, create daily lists of Things to Do.

Filing documents

In tray for bills to be paid. Filing bills and important documents in folders or ring binders.

Physical Care

Hair cut, massage, chiropractor, dentist, doctor, exercise machine or exercise club.

Clothes

Buying, laundering or dry cleaning, ironing, mending, storage – both casual and work clothes.

Financial

Expenditure chart (incoming and outgoings), paying bills on time, checking the efficiency of your expenditure. Filing bank statements, invoices, receipts, guarantees etc.

Home

Keeping your home clean and tidy. Maintenance for intruder alarm, gas fires, boiler, fire detectors, fire extinguishers in working order, maintaining roof, and outside of building.

Car

Regular maintenance and safety checks, car insurance and licence kept up-to-date.

Work

Organised filing system, portfolio, product samples, printed advertising material, business cards. Also appropriate work clothes kept in good order.

Keeping tidy and use of good storage

Basically, everything you own needs a home, or else it becomes a weed, (something not in the right place). Identify belongings that don't have a home and create a place for them. You may need to have a clear-out to create more space. Prioritise, if you mentally group and divide your possessions into: "used every day", "used sometimes", "rarely used" and "keepsakes" then simply give priority of prime space to the things you use the most.

Make a list of any 'homeless' possessions and then decide where their homes will be from now on. Create archive boxes to put away things you rarely use. If you don't have space maybe you could consider outsourcing storage requirements.

Organising Tracking Chart

Now you have identified problem areas that need organising you can complete the Organising Tracking Chart.

You need to ensure that you have organised yourself and that you have a proper place for all your belongings, and pertinent information.

Write down the problem area, followed by what you are going to do to improve in that area. Following is an example Organising Tracking Chart. You can then fill in your own chart, for whichever areas need addressing.

Free templates for this exercise are available on our website:

www.theachieversjourney.com

Example - Organising Tracking Chart

Identified problem area's that need organising	Solution to implement change	Date I will implement this change (Put reminder of this in diary!)	Completed Task (tick)
Diary	Buy a diary and enter appointments and prompts to do things	Get a diary today whilst out shopping	
Sort my old clothes	Sort out clothes take to charity shop	This weekend	
Ski wear	Put in suitcase that's in the loft	This weekend	
Books	New bookshelf for the study -	Weekend of the 28th 29th May	
File Important documents	Create important document file, put in bottom drawer of study	This weekend	
Keepsakes	Get storage container, name the container Prepare inventory list for the loft	Complete in week off work in June	
Household bills	Create folders and update regularly	Prioritise what needs doing now. Complete during week off in June	

Organising Tracking Chart

Identified problem area's that need organising	Solution to implement change	Date I will implement this change (Put reminder of this in diary!)	Completed Task (tick)

Further help on finding solutions and implementing change

I will now provide general advice on organising, to help you with implementing changes to the unruly, unorganised areas of your life. Where this has been applicable, clients often report that they really benefit from this part of mentoring.

Keeping records

We all need to keep good records. Below are methods for achieving this.

Being dyslexic I have to try and keep myself very organised. Dyslexic or not, your life could dramatically improve once you get yourself properly organised.

Let's look at financial records overleaf.

Financial Records

It is essential that you keep track of your financial incomings and outgoings. To help you with this I have devised a simple basic Financial Tracking Chart. The following sample chart is January through June you can use the same chart and label it July to December. It doesn't matter if you update it electronically or manually as long as it is updated.

Example - Financial Tracking Chart

Details of expense	Budget Jan	Actual Jan	Budget Feb	Actual Feb	Budget March	Actual March	Budget April	Actual April	Budget May	Actual May	Budget June	Actual June
Mortgage	$1,000	$1,000	$1,000	$1,000	$1,000	$1,050	$1,050	$1,050	$1,050	$1,050	$1,050	$1,050
Council tax	$50	$50	$50	$60	$60	$60	$60	$60	$60	$60	$60	$60
Electric	$30	$30	$30	$30	$30	$30	$30	$30	$30	$30	$30	$30
Car fuel	$120	$120	$120	$120	$120	$120	$130	$130	$130	$130	$130	$130
Etc												
Total												

Chapter Seven - Being Organised 115

Financial Tracking Chart

Details of expense	Budget	Actual	Budget	Actual	Budget	Actual	Budget	Actual	Budget	Actual	Budget	Actual	Budget	Actual
Total														

Records (continued)

Diary

Using and regularly updating your diary is essential to being organised. Choose a method that is right for you, either electronic or hard copy, and remember to keep it updated. Record appointments and holidays in advance.

Data bases

Data bases are also important to being organised, select the best system for your needs. I personally keep an electronic as well as hard copy (printout) of all my data. Make sure your data is correct before recording it to avoid inaccurate or incomplete information. Do take the time to record everything correctly and regularly update it.

I have also divided my data bases into different areas of my life: friends and family, health practitioners, service providers, etc.

Do make sure all your data is kept in a safe place. To be safe, print out copies and also keep a back-up disk of all the data. I also cross-shred all my papers before sending for recycling.

Organising tips for making life easier

Over the years I have had to find alternative ways of doing certain everyday tasks. For certain things it takes me a lot longer to do than the average person, but I have developed ways to cope with my dyslexia, methods that have also helped thousands of others and I would like to share them with you.

Highlighting numbers and words

On the upside, I take in and process information quickly, and add and subtract numbers in my head well, the challenge is that I cannot identify text and numbers instantly on a

Chapter Seven - Being Organised

page or computer screen. Without being able to read the data, I can't read most spreadsheets, invoices, statements, etc. For me it's like looking at Chinese, a language I don't understand. I used to always get someone else to read them for me. However, when I progressed into senior management in one of the world's largest corporations, I soon realised I would have to find a different way around such problems.

So I reverted back to a method my parents had devised for me as a child for seeing numbers — colours! I got my P.A. to use different highlighter pens for different items. Each spreadsheet would be prepared this way, and when I went into a meeting, I could then keep up with everyone else. For example the sub-totals were highlighted in pink and the gross amounts in green.

I am not ashamed nor embarrassed about being dyslexic and dyspraxic, and advised the Board that when reading most documents I used a ruler to follow the text, and for financial material I used colour coding. Everyone accepted this, and all was fine.

Over the following weeks however, I noticed that my colleagues were starting to use my colour coding, even in the Finance Department. How kind, I thought, that people were doing this for me, just in case I needed to be looking at the documents. However, when I brought the matter up at the next Board meeting, all admitted that they had taken up the colour coding because it made their lives so much easier as well.

Memory Statements

My long term memory is great: if you name any date in my life since I was three I will tell you what I was doing and all the colours of the wallpaper in my home at that time. But my short term memory isn't quite so good. I often put things down and can't find them again, especially my car keys. So, what I do now is say out loud, "putting car keys on kitchen work surface," and somehow that penetrates my mind and I know exactly where they are later when I need them. I have given lots of other people this method, and it nearly always works.

Organising - having everything you need

I try and make my life easier whenever I can. I have my main home on the South coast of England just up from the beach, which I love, and we have a flat and an office in the heart of London (equally as exciting), which is used about four days per week. We also travel abroad extensively.

Can you imagine what organising that takes? So what I have done is duplicate all the things I need, for several locations. I have an identical bathroom cabinet and drawers in the house and flat, which hold identical items, including: toiletries, medication, first aid kit, umbrella, make-up, tooth brush, etc. For travelling I have a big cosmetic case with the same things. I even have insert drawers that fit into my suitcase, so when I arrive at a destination I just slot them into the drawers in the hotel or cabin bedroom. In the car and in the office I have a smaller version of the same, just in case I have to go somewhere fast. So when I buy something I simply buy four, it makes for a much easier life.

Take a look at your life, find what needs organising, (or re-organising), write it down, then plan and implement changes accordingly.

Make lists

Whenever you need to remember something you want to get or do, use a sheet of paper or notebook to jot it down. None of us remember everything all the time and lists are so useful. For some things you can also start a list and just keep adding to it.

My favourite lists include the one on the back of my door in the kitchen of reminders of vital things for any trip, including purse, mobile phone and its adapter, credit cards, etc.

Diaries, calendars and wall planners

Diaries, calendars and planners are great tools for keeping you organised. Discover which method of recording data works best for you. My work and holidays abroad are scheduled about eighteen months in advance, so I have a planner to see quickly where I am going to be and when.

Visual reminders

Another one of my parents' strategies was to write down things I was trying to learn on sheets of paper and put them on the wall. Mine had to be colour-coded, but yours probably won't need to be.

My multiplication tables were put up opposite my bed, and each night I would look at them. Eventually, these numbers penetrated my mind. You too can use this method - to learn different languages, formulas, etc. I do the same in my office. I have many treasured staff, and service providers, whose names I am familiar with, but the new ones I can't remember names for, so I write them where I can see them. Eventually, they seem to penetrate my mind so that I can ensure I get the names right when I need them.

Prioritising

Prioritising is a problem for most people. This is an exercise to help you re-assess your priorities by tracking your responsibilities and commitments.

List your responsibilities and commitments and review them. Then decide whether to retain them, reassess them or delegate them in part or full.

Responsibilities and Commitment Sheet

Responsibility and/or commitment	Is it realistic?	Keep it? Re-assess it? Delegate some responsibility?

Creating good balance in your life

Do you have good balance in your life? Let's review some sections of your life. Highlight the areas that need addressing, you might want to add them to your Organising Chart.

Do you:

    1. have adequate sleep?

    2. buy and prepare healthy food?

    3. take time to eat regularly and properly?

    4. take regular exercise?

    5. find ways to be productive at work?

    6. take time to socialise with family and friends?

    7. update you skill sets and education?

    8. deal with your finances properly?

    9. take time out to relax?

    10. take regular breaks and holidays?

    11. have regular health checks: doctors and dentists?

Good division of time

We are now going to review how you divide your time. Over the course of your life you evolve and change. You consistently make decisions and re-adjustments on how much time is spent on each activity as you continue to assess (or re-assess) your priorities.

Good time-management

Good time management isn't just if you arrive early, on time, or late for appointments it's how has your division of time changed over the years? If you are always late is there a reason behind this? Do you need to review your division of time in your life?

If this is something that you feel that you should address then this section could help you.

You could estimate your division of time, but for a better idea you could do this exercise to see how you actually spend your time, over the course of a week or a month, on different things, and then analyse it properly.

You can do the exercise in this book or in your notebook or A4 ring binder.

The chart can be used for any aspect of your life, for a week, a month, or more. Fill in the day and date followed by what you did and how much time was spent on it.

Often my clients get such a shock when they realise how they divide their time, as they have no idea how out of balance they have become.

Time allocation is very individual, and yours should be specifically tailored to your own needs and preferences. Prioritise on important time division. Obviously not every second should be counted as you may be travelling, shopping and completing many daily tasks. But track the division of times that are important to you.

Chapter Seven - Being Organised

Example - Division of Time Chart

Person who is self employed

Action	Good balance would be?	Day 1 (actual)	Day 2 (actual)	Day 3 (actual)	Day 4 (actual)	Day 5 (actual)	Day 6 (actual)	Day 7 (actual)
Sleep	8 hrs Per day	6hrs	6hrs	6hrs	7hrs	5hrs	6hrs	8hrs
Time with children	3 hrs Per day	1hr	1hr	1hr	1hr	1hr	4hrs	8hrs
Buy & prepare healthy food	1 hr Per day	1 hr	0 hr	0 hr	0 hr	0 hr	1 hr	0 hr
Exercise	1hr Per day	1hr	0 hr	0 hr	0 hr	0 hr	0 hr	1 hr
Work (Self employed person)	8hrs Per day mon-fri	9 hrs Monday	9 hrs Tuesday	9 hrs Wed	9 hrs Thurs	9 hrs Fri	6 hrs Sat	3 hrs Sun
Socialising	7 hrs per week	0 hrs	0 hrs	0 hrs	0hrs	1hrs	2 hrs	1 hr
Further Education	2 hrs per week	0 hrs	0 hrs	0 hrs	0 hrs	0 hrs	0 hrs	0 hrs

Chapter Seven - Being Organised

Division of Time Chart

Action	Good balance?	Day 1 (actual)	Day 2 (actual)	Day 3 (actual)	Day 4 (actual)	Day 5 (actual)	Day 6 (actual)	Day 7 (actual)

Chapter Seven - Being Organised

Divisions of Time

Some clients have liked this exercise where you write down in percentage terms how your life has been divided up in an average week, at different stages in your life.

As you do this, it is interesting to see how you have evolved in your division of time, and keep re-evaluating as your life enters different phases.

You can do the exercise for any age you choose. Look back at your results from when you were eight. Was your life more balanced as a child, when other people balanced it for you, and before you gained more responsibility?

If you don't have a balanced life now, why is that?

Is the imbalance your fault? Or do you feel it's someone else's?

To stay organised with your division of time you need to regularly review how you divide your time, and adjust it accordingly.

With our busy lives, we regularly underestimate how much time we need for all the things we want to do. Too often we leave no margins, and when just one thing changes, there is no room for manoeuvre. Time is pinched from another area and as a result our diet and sleep often suffer.

Be realistic, cut the cloth adequately, leaving some space to manoeuvre should you need to.

Chapter Seven - Being Organised

Division of Time Chart

	At 8 years old	At 16 years old	When you started Work	Time division 5 years ago	Time division now
Sleeping					
Preparing Food					
Eating					
Exercising					
Working					
Socialising					
Education					
Relaxing					

Division of time in difficult circumstances
Self nurturing

Sometimes we can't control the events in our life. But if division of time is too unbalanced you may become physically out of balance, or unwell because of it. Poor time management is neither good for you, nor for other people in your life. You need to take stock, stand back and think about what is going to work best for you, in your present situation.

If you are experiencing difficult circumstances, you can still make healthy choices about your division of time and find time to nurture yourself.

I can personally appreciate that it is very difficult to try to plan and look forward, during difficult times in your life.

I lost my last remaining grandparent, my grandfather, my beloved parents to cancer and a brain tumour, one after another, then unbelievably only months after their death, I lost my only sibling, my much-loved bachelor brother was found dead in his flat, from a heart attack, at the age of thirty seven. With the exception of my husband and daughter, I lost my whole immediate family in the space of four years.

Also during this time I had been undergoing IVF treatment, and sadly lost triplets in early pregnancy.

It sounds strange but I felt far too young for all this to be happening to me. We all lose loved ones in life but I had always thought I would be older when this happened. I was devastated. I felt crushed. I simply couldn't cope. Every day I was fearful of what else this cruel life could throw at me. I suffered terrible depression.

My doctor told me that to get over all these awful events the only way through was to self-nurture; I had been so tied up with everyone else that I had stopped nurturing

Chapter Seven - Being Organised

and looking after myself. When I was running on empty I wasn't able to help myself or anyone else because I was in such a low state.

I began to look at the difficulties, plan goals and then implement them. I decided to concentrate on my diet, exercises and set small goals to accomplish for each day. My priority was my daughter. I accepted help from my best friend Mandy and Heather, who among other things, took my daughter to school each day. They helped enormously.

I also decided to take short breaks and holidays, which often are very beneficial when I am feeling low. Eventually, with two steps forward and one back, I gradually achieved and went forward into a new chapter. We moved to a lovely house in a country location, our business grew strongly as did our new edition, a beautiful puppy called Millie. During this difficult time being organised made life a lot easier.

Now lets move on to how you can create ways to make life easier for yourself and those around you.

Progress Report:

You have made excellent progress in this chapter by getting yourself organised. You have:

- ❏ *identified the areas in your life that are not well organised.*

- ❏ *had the opportunity to complete an Organising Tracking Chart that will help you implement better organisation*

- ❏ *had the opportunity to fill in your Personal Financial Chart, if you haven't got one already*

- ❏ *considered prioritising things in your life*

- ❏ *looked at maintaining good balance and division of time in your life*

- ❏ *received tips on keeping things neat and tidy*

- ❏ *realised the benefits of self nurturing*

At this point of your journey:

- *Do you want to chart any progress to your original map or create a new map to explain where you are? (optional)*

- *Having completed this chapter are there any notes you wish to enter in your note book?*

- *Are there amendments to what you have listed as your initial goals: short, medium or long term?*

Chapter Eight

Keep up the Performance

Don't look back - unless that's the way you intend to go...

What miles we have now travelled together!

On this journey you have learnt a lot of new skill sets, you've identified problems, difficulties, and any bad habits. You have created goals, implemented and tracked them. You have made a conscious effort to take responsibility by charting your own course and planning your own brighter future - rather than standing still.

Along the way you have come to know yourself better, and hopefully adopted effective new ways of motivating yourself, through tracking and being more organised.

In this the final chapter of my mentoring in this book, as

you travel on, and as I now evolve from passenger and guide to a friend you can always re-acquaint yourself with, I want to give you ideas on how to successfully keep up your excellent performance.

To do this you need to keep moving forward, use the many exercises and teachings you have learnt on this particular journey, and remember to collect and treasure all your successes as you travel.

Recording your achievements

During my lifetime it has never failed to astound me just how much people underestimate, fail to treasure, or even remember the successes that they have achieved in their lives.

Each and every one of us has had successes, however, too often we either don't see them for what they are or, if we do acknowledge them at the time, we soon forget. On a bad day we can feel that we never achieve anything at all, which isn't true, or doubt ourselves and our abilities.

Success and achievements are earned - they don't just happen

When you have achieved something, treasure it forever. Find a way of making a trophy to remember it. You could put a photo of it up on the wall, write it down, or anything that helps you to remember and re-live the memory.

The feeling of really achieving something and feeling successful should be enjoyed and reflected on throughout your life. The more important ones should be celebrated, and shared with the younger members of your family, to inspire them on their journeys. Children should constantly get praise and acknowledgement of achievements from different sources: parents, guardians, teachers, sports coaches, etc.

Chapter Eight - Keep up the Performance

I want you to treasure all that you have accomplished on this journey.

When you're an adult you have to make note of your own successes because you don't get the same praise, from as many other sources as when you were a child. If you don't record your achievements, chances are no one else will.

Praise, in whatever form, is important. Each day record in your exercise book small achievements, nice comments, or compliments you receive.

Having achievements recognised

It is vital to have achievements recognised. Additionally, we must try and accept others who have difficulties, whatever they are, and acknowledge their successes too, whatever they may be. Success for some can often be simply making an effort to do something new.

If you are a manager of people, if you are involved with children, and even with your partner, remember to give praise where it is due. Also remember to give self praise.

You must never give up on trying. My Mum used to say, "There is no such thing as can't". I believe any successes in my life are simply because I never stopped trying. Indeed, early learning and school could be described as a 'an ongoing challenge'. But with perseverance and developing my other gifts, and with the help of computers, by my twenties I started to write much better. (The computer greatly improves my spelling and grammar.)

By my mid-twenties, I was working in quite high-powered jobs and earning far more than my peers. For the last decade I have run successful businesses, have worked all over the world, enjoying a fabulous life style.

Once, people thought I would never be able to read or write

fully. Today I write books, narrate, and am a professional mentor. If I can do it, anyone can.

I believe that there is an author in all of us. If you feel there is a book in you, don't be frightened, you just need to find your own way through the process. It doesn't have to be published work. You can leave your memoirs and your achievements for your children and grandchildren, or keep a diary. However you choose to record your message or story, just do it, for what you don't record now will be lost forever.

Exercise

Your achievements to-date

When clients do this exercise, they often start off by listing educational qualifications, obtained over a short period of their lives - which in some cases could have been 20 years ago.

Then I say to them, "So you achieved nothing before or since these qualifications?" In response they add passing their driving test. Eventually I get them to write down all their accomplishments, and they are usually amazed at the amount of things they have actually done. Sometimes it's the small things that mean the most.

Not all achievements are necessarily successes, but things you achieved because you made the effort.

I want you to have a good think and write down *all* your achievements and then remember to add to the list as you achieve even more.

Chapter Eight - Keep up the Performance

Your personal achievements

Achievements are what you put effort into!

Make a note of all your past achievements. The following prompters may help, and are deliberately not in any particular order. Bear in mind that a huge achievement for one person can be a simple chore for someone else; we are all different in our abilities and rate of progress.

If you get stuck, try asking someone close to you for their ideas.

View these examples and then create your own list.

Made the effort to move on

Held down a job

Recovered from an illness, or accident

Conquered an addiction

Survived abuse

Coped with physical or mental difficulties

Learned to read and write

Made the effort to keep yourself fit

Got on a plane or transport that you used to dread

Dealt with grief

Overcame negative comments received in the past

Coped with terminal illness

Coped with being a carer

Picked yourself up when you felt life was against you, and started again

Got over a trauma and came out the other side

Dealt with a legal battle

Got over a fear

Learned to swim

Passed exams

Created a garden

Painted a picture

Learned to take photographs

Designed a web site

Decorated a house/flat

Purchased my own home

Purchased my first or a special car, boat or plane!

Raised kids – being parent or guardian

Went through a pregnancy, gave birth!!

Being a good partner

Survived divorce

Survived redundancy

Dealt with depression or a breakdown

Obtained a new job

Started a business

Succeeded and achieved at job – promotion

Successfully self-employed

Passed driving test

Adapted to difficult change in life

Resolved issues with friends or family

Attempted to run a marathon or raising money for good causes

Saved peoples lives by your actions or your job

Improved other peoples' quality of life

Cared for the elderly

You may also want to include all the countries and destinations that you have been to; each trip is an achievement.

Once you have made your list, keep adding to it and keep this ongoing, life-long list either in your personal notebook or on your computer.

Chapter Eight - Keep up the Performance

My Personal Achievement Chart

List your personal achievements in any order that you like

Factors/Conditions that help personal achievement

Take a good look at your achievements. Are there any factors that affected a successful outcome that might help you in the future? For example, looking at my achievements I can see many different patterns that helped me achieve. This included continuing to make an effort. I am also more successful if I plan my goals, motivate myself and allow a realistic time frame to achieve it, prior to implementing it. Also, it's amazing that I can find extra motivation for losing that extra bit of weight I'm carrying when I am due to go on holiday or have a wedding to go to!

I have witnessed other people achieving well after finding themselves in an unexpected situation, or after a life-changing experience. Following are just some of the most common factors or conditions, (yours may differ). See if you can identify any that may help with your future goals.

- ❏ *Choosing the right time to implement your goals*
- ❏ *Being more determined*
- ❏ *Being motivated by your family or friends*
- ❏ *Being motivated by an unexpected situation*
- ❏ *Being motivated by a forthcoming event*
- ❏ *Enlisting other people to help with your goal(s)*
- ❏ *Choosing the right time of year eg. New year – Keeping to New Years resolutions*
- ❏ *Moving away from negative circumstances*
- ❏ *Creating new environment at home or work*
- ❏ *Making the most of an opportunity*
- ❏ *Progressing after a health scare*
- ❏ *Working on staying positive*

If there are patterns emerging from your achievements, be aware of these and use them if you can for your goals in the future.

Chapter Eight - Keep up the Performance

Talking of achievements, I have to say, Well done! You have reached the conclusion of this book/journey. However, the journey continues as many new paths, roads and valleys lie before you, but now you are better informed and able to chart your own course and look forward to exciting new horizons.

That just leaves me to say it has been a great privilege to have shared in your personal journey. I invite you to re-visit, and get re-inspired, any time you wish.

Until we meet again, have a wonderful journey…

Long may you achieve,

Yours -

Genevieve Dawid

Resources

Updated relevant resource information details are provided on our website.

www.theachieversjouney.com

Mentoring Courses

For more information on Mentoring courses

By Genevieve Dawid

Either One to One mentoring,

Interactive Workshops, Seminars

or courses held in wonderful locations worldwide

View our website at

www.theachieversjourney.com

Keynote speeches

For more information on keynote speeches

by Genevieve Dawid

View our website at

www.genevievedawid.com

ISBN 978-0-9556529-0-5